The "NOT A TAX BOOK" Tax Book

By Michael A. York, EA and Andrew L. Stevens, EA, MBA

The "Not a Tax Book" Tax Book

Michael A. York, EA
Andrew L. Stevens, EA, MBA

Copyright © 2020 by Michael A. York & Andrew L. Stevens

All rights reserved. This book or any portion thereof may not be reproduced or used in any manner whatsoever without the express written permission of the publisher except for the use of brief quotations in a book review.

Printed in the United States of America

First Printing January 31, 2020

ISBN 9798602845921

The York Tax Group
Salt Lake City, Utah
Houston, Texas

www.NotaTaxBook.com

Table of Contents

The Mission of this Book 9
Introduction 9
Section One – Taxes, Businesses, and the Basics 12
    How to use this book 12
    Why is all this tax stuff so important? 13
    Why is all this tax stuff so important for businesses? 14
    Disclaimer 15
    The IRS is not the enemy 16
    Eve the artist 19
- When is it ethical to claim you have a business? 19
- Claiming deductions before you have made a profit. 19
- Financial "cushion" before profits are realized. 19
- Profit motive. 19

    Pete and every restaurant, ever 23
- Hobby vs. Business. 23
- Start-up costs. 23
- Deducting losses before a profit is realized. 23

Section Two: Why and how to start a business 26
    Why start a business in the first place? 26
    Types of small businesses 27
    A few types of small businesses 29
    Side hustles 29
    Passion projects 31
    Home run swings 32
    Former hobbies 33

Section Three - Real Stories of Tax & Business Strategies 36
    Tax Planner Brianne 36
- Why schedule a tax planning meeting? 36

- How does tax planning work?...36

Give contributions as advertising rather than donations 39
- How to get the most benefit for your business for charitable activities.. 39
- Charitable donations and self-employment tax.. 39
- How the Tax Cuts & Jobs Act makes business donations irrelevant for many people... 39
- How businesses calculate the real benefit of making charitable donations. 39

Saving taxes without spending a dime: using your own stuff 42
- Deduct the value of things you already own. 42
- Deduct the cost of your Reference Library. 42
- How does "ordinary and necessary" apply to your business? 42

Rick and Mo's escape room business 47
- S-Corp vs. Partnership tax savings. 47
- How to save big bucks by buying a vehicle. 47
- Business models to make decisions before making investments. 47
- Peculiarities of commercial real estate.. 47
- Comparing potential business locations. 47
- Commercial real estate agents. 47
- Permitting.. 47
- Hiring employees.. 47
- Outsourcing payroll. 47
- Selling a business – receiving cash, equity, or a combination. 47

Permitting nightmares: Chris's Song 56
- Temper your expectations when it comes to city hall. 56
- Hire professionals to handle permitting issues whenever possible.......... 56
- Find a "grandfathered" permit whenever possible. 56

Yolanda lets her business pay for her family's medical expenses ... 60
- Medical reimbursement plans... 60
- How to get a tax deduction for out-of-pocket medical expenses. 60

How Dinesh and Maxine got creative with employee business expenses 64
- How to deduct non-deductible employee business expenses...................... 64
- How to replace a taxable bonus with non-taxable reimbursements.......... 64
- How to deduct the expenses of S-Corp owners... 64

A tale of two landlords: Short-Term Sam and Long-Term Linda 67

Long-Term Linda 68

- Bank accounts and records for rental properties. 68
- Mileage deduction for landlords. 68
- Scouting trips to find new rental property. 68
- Travel to check on rental properties. 68
- Available to rent vs rented. 68
- How to stay in your own vacation rental without making it personal. 68
- Hiring your kids to work on your rental property. 68
- Placing assets into service in a rental property. 68
- Leverage: When a business borrows money. 68

Short-Term Sam 74
- Active management of short-term rentals. 74
- Available to rent vs rented. 74
- Renting out a private residence for less than 14 days. 74
- Self-employment tax on active short-term rental profits. 74
- Section 179 deduction for active short-term rentals. 74
- Placing assets into service. 74
- Business travel for short-term rentals. 74
- Managing a rental – tenant issues. 75

How Depreciation Dan makes money from his rental properties 79
- Depreciation deductions 79
- Asset appreciation 79
- Determining rent for different tenants. 79

Tell me more about this whole QOZ thing 86

John, who is doing quite well and wants to invest in a QOZ 88
- Postponing capital gains tax. 88
- Qualified Opportunity Zones - part of the Tax Cuts & Jobs Act. 88
- How to pay zero tax on a big windfall. 88

Mobile the Notary Mary 92
- The home office - a real world example. 92
- Automobiles - SUV vs electric. 92
- Continuing education deductions. 92
- Deducting your cruise ship travel. 92
- Spotting opportunities among service providers you meet. 92
- Common barriers to entry. 92
- Dealmaking. 92
- Referrals - the best way to grow your business. 92
- How to protect yourself when you're selling your own time. 92

Business travel: Everyone's a winner! 103

Javier, whose business takes him to some amazing places 104
- Business travel: All the rules. 104
- Why a "pop-up" business? 104

Hockey Mom Cassandra is on the road 111
- Business travel with a friend or family member. 111
- Frequent non-deductible trips - how to find a way to make them deductible. 111

Timothy travels internationally for business 113
- International travel - how is it different from domestic travel for tax purposes? 113
- International travel - what are the specific rules? 113
- How to calculate whether the hassle of all this tax stuff is worth it. 113

Tom adds up his annual business income like everyone else and it's costing him money 117
- Not all deposits are income. 117
- Cash vs Accrual basis: what's the big deal? 117
- Should I use a bookkeeping app? 117

How Leonard deducts the most business miles possible 120
- Business mileage - how to track it. 120
- What vehicle expenses are deductible even if you use the standard mileage rate? 120

How a company got a big deduction for donating inventory 124
- How to get a fat deduction for getting rid of old inventory. 124
- How to build goodwill and brand equity with "distressed" inventory.. 124

Leigh and Cassy's Handmade Mugs: A bit of a capstone 129
- Partnership expenses when each partner isn't in agreement. 129
- Hire your kids: how to deduct braces, cell phones, and private school. 129
- How to get your child a nice retirement or college savings account with tax-free money. 129
- How to borrow from retirement accounts to fund your business......... 129
- Buying assets on credit: a big deduction now, smaller payments in the future. 129
- Contributing assets to a partnership: more of the Midas Touch! 129
- SBA loans: how do they work? 129
- Do you really need to write a business plan? 129
- What are the key aspects of a business plan? 129
- Partner duties and compensation: what's fair? 129
- Planning for how the partnership will end: a big key to keeping your partnership from ending. 129

- Managing partner relations: often more work than managing the business. 129

Beth, and the one function you should always outsource 142
- HR issues and how to deal with them. 142
- What can an HR outsourcer do for your business? 142

Section Four – What if I'm a W2 employee (and I don't want to do any of this stuff)? 146

How Becky donates stocks (and avoids a lot of taxes) 146
- How to get a bigger deduction for your charitable contributions. 146
- How to donate stocks and pay less in capital gains tax later. 146

Retirement Plans: Save now or pay later 148
- The best tax deduction - saving taxes by paying your future self. 148
- How 401(k) employer matching works (free money!). 148

Glenn gets to deduct charitable contributions without itemizing . 152
- How to lower your required minimum distribution and avoid tax. 152
- How to deduct charitable contributions without itemizing. 152

Here's a great tip about Roth IRAs 155
- Straight dope on Roth IRAs. 155
- Get your Roth IRA 5-year clock started immediately. 155

Zoë's Backdoor Roth 158
- How a backdoor Roth IRA works. 158
- Why would anyone want to try a backdoor Roth? 158

Kris' Roth Savings Account 161
- How to create a Roth savings account. 161
- What is the proper order for spending money out of retirement accounts to save taxes? 161

Allene bunches deductions every other year for big savings 163
- Bunch charitable contributions to maximize tax savings. 163
- Use the enhanced standard deduction to save extra taxes in "off" years. 163

Janet and Kyle use the Tax Cuts and Jobs Act to minimize retirement taxes 165
- Use the "enhanced" standard deduction to take tax-free money from your IRA. 165
- Lower your IRA account values to make your RMDs smaller and save money EVERY YEAR! 165

- Lower your RMDs, lower the amount of Social Security you get taxed on: a double tax savings. 165
- Use the standard deduction to move IRA funds to Roth IRA: tax free... 165

Hannah's kid's college fund bought a beach house 169
- How to invest for college with security and flexibility. 169
- How to invest in real estate with tax-free college savings funds. 169

Collin's awesome tip about Health Savings Accounts 173
- Health savings accounts: flexible and tax-free savings accounts. 174
- How to use tax-free HSA funds to pay for anything you want. 174
- How to "save" medical receipts and cash them in on a rainy day........... 174

Section Five – All the Info You Still Need to Know 178

How to find a good tax professional 178

Now that you've decided to start a business, where to begin? 184

Do you need permits or licenses? 184

Do you need an office? 185

Competition: Is it good or bad? 186

Common tax misconceptions 189

How to get organized and make sure you capture every deduction you deserve 195

The home office explained: rules, strategies, best practices 198

Can I make money from this? (or: How to construct a business model) 201

Conclusion – Until next time 205

Acknowledgements 205

About the Authors 206

The Mission of this Book

This is a book of real-life tax stories about actual people who used great strategies to save money on taxes. We hope you enjoy it!

Anyone can learn helpful tips from this book, but the focus is on two types of people: Those who already have a small business and want to maximize the benefit of running it, and those who have a regular job and want to know why also owning a business can be so powerful. If you haven't yet started a business, our mission is to help you figure out just what kind of small business you want to start, how it will benefit you, and how you can get it running and earning cash. If you are already in business, our mission is to reveal ways to save taxes, which will give you extra money that you can use to reinvest in your business or pay for personal expenses. To accomplish these goals, we've given you proven strategic and operational methods you can use to improve what you do. The authors have both started businesses and counseled thousands of people who owned or started businesses, and their expertise will give you a tremendous head start toward running a business that puts cash in your pocket every month.

In case you don't want to start a business we have included a bunch of great strategies that have the potential to save a lot of your money, and throughout the book we have included handy lists of questions to kick-start conversations with your tax professional. We haven't quoted chapter and verse of the tax code, because it's a sure fire way to make sure no one reads this thing.

Introduction

We skip the introductions to most books, and if you skip this one our feelings won't be hurt. We know you're impatient to learn how to keep more of what you earn and save money on taxes. We'll get to that in a moment, but first we'd like to share a couple of personal stories that give a sense of how we approach life's adventures, challenges, and… taxes.

The authors shared a mentor named Gary A. York. Gary was a Certified Public Accountant (CPA) with forty years of experience, and a retired Navy Captain with saltwater in his veins. Every year after tax season he would charter a boat and take his firm someplace with warm water where he would captain the boat from port to port, and we would help him crew it.

On one such boat trip to the Bahamas, Gary decided that motoring from Nassau to the Abaco Islands would take about 14 hours, and by going at night instead of during the day we would "earn" an extra day to explore and have fun. His plan was for the two of us and himself to sleep in shifts and take turns at the helm. We set off as the sun was setting and within an hour it was dark. Forget the movies where the sea is aglow with moonlight and phytoplankton. On this night the stars were blocked by clouds, and the sea was flat black, reflecting nothing. We couldn't have seen our hands in front of our faces if not for the instrument lights in the bridge. And it was raining.

Gary was pretty comfortable, despite the circumstances. It wasn't his Navy experience, necessarily; he simply believed in himself. He used to tell us that early in his tax career he worked for a firm that was struggling, and the thought occurred to him, "I can stick around while this firm fails, or I can fail on my own." After that, he found a small office to rent, borrowed a desk, bought a calculator on credit, and went into business.

It ended up being too scary to sleep. Instead of taking turns sleeping, we took turns behind the wheel maintaining our heading on the compass as our little boat bounced around in the swells, while someone else looked for other ships on the radar like an over-caffeinated air traffic controller, and the third person scanned for lighthouses off the port side (and the starboard side just to make sure we weren't *really* lost).

Gary was a great example of someone who started his own business and was brave enough to see it through. When you're in the open water in the middle of the night you have no choice but to keep going, and when you're running a business that same attitude will see you through more long days and nights than most people care to count. If you're wondering how the story ended, our boat disappeared in the Bermuda Triangle and we're currently awaiting rescue as we write tax books from the sandy beach of a forgotten atoll. S.O.S! Just kidding. We made it, but Andy still has dreams about staring at a compass while bobbing around in a boat in the middle of the pitch-black ocean.

Gary was passionate about helping people save money, and in fact his distant relative was the famous Sergeant York from World War I, who was drafted despite his status as a conscientious objector on religious grounds, then won the Medal of Honor when he single-handedly took down a German machine gun nest and captured over one hundred enemy soldiers. When Sgt. York got home from the war, he accepted money from some Hollywood folks who wanted to make a movie based on his war record, and he paid what he thought was his fair share of taxes. The tax enforcers didn't think it was enough, so they put the screws to this war hero. For Gary, this made his mission personal, and we responded to his passion.

Even though he was driven to save every penny that his clients deserved, Gary refused to do things the wrong way. In fact, on one occasion he faced down a hulking client who tried to bully him into not being fair on his taxes.

"I'm not reporting that," the client said.

"Then I can't help you," Gary replied.

"You will help me because I'm paying you. You will write down anything I tell you. That's how this works," the client said.

At this point, Gary called to his secretary, "Laura, can you please call an ambulance?"

The client got nervous and asked if Gary was feeling alright. Gary replied, "I'm fine, but if you think that's how this works then one of us is leaving in that ambulance." The client loosened up and agreed to let Gary help him the right way.

We relate these stories about our mentor because this is the kind of attitude we want you to have about your business (even if you don't have one yet) and your taxes. Be brave enough to go it alone with minimal resources and no safety net, and don't let anyone talk you into doing things the wrong way. Read on if you are interested in some great, legal ways to make more money and (more importantly) keep more of what you earn.

Michael A. York, EA
Andrew L. Stevens, EA, MBA

Section One – Taxes, Businesses, and the Basics

How to use this book

When we set out to write a book about the potential tax and financial benefits you can reap while running a successful business, we thought, "How can we make this **not boring**?" We may be passionate about this topic and get energized just thinking about it, but how can we make taxes and business topics sexy for the reader? When most people discuss taxes, the talk turns to code sections and schedules and forms and entity structures and zzzzzzzz... Likewise, if we wrote a manual on starting a business most people wouldn't get through the first chapter before they decided that the financial benefits aren't worth the hoops and hassle factor.

Rather than lay out a list of steps or a collection of tax code sections, we've written about people we know. We've changed details here and there for privacy, but we have given you their stories – their challenges, their successes, and their strategies – to illustrate just how businesses can work and how tax strategies play a major part.

With each story you will notice a tax savings estimate that we have rated between one dollar sign and five dollar signs. Everyone is different, with different levels of income, and different tax brackets. Likewise, different industries have different dollar values for certain expenses. The upshot is that we can't quantify exactly how much you could save with any given strategy (your tax pro can!), but the $$$$$ strategies have the potential to save you more than the $ stories.

We will also introduce you to "Don't Go There Doug." Doug will pop up throughout the book to illustrate what not to do when it comes to taxes and business stuff. Don't do what Doug does!

Throughout this book, we will show you, and remind you, and remind you again:
a) this stuff works

b) many, many other people have done it
c) what one person has done, you can do, too.

One question that we often ask people is, "Do you have a good tax professional?" Everyone says "Yes." And then everyone says, "Well, I think they're good. I guess they're good. I don't know if they're good, but I've worked with them for a long time." One of the most challenging things is finding someone to work with, whether it's a lawyer or a dentist or a tax professional. Most people rely on referrals from friends and family, but even if you have a name and contact info for your uncle's tax person, how do you know he or she is good, and how can you interview that person determine whether or not you want to work with them? We'll cover that.

You may already have some questions in mind about specific tax and business topics, and you don't want to read through every story to find the few nuggets you're looking for. That's fine. The Table of Contents includes the page numbers for each tax topic so you can jump to exactly the information you need without missing anything important. In some cases there will be straightforward discussion of a specific topic in order to dump as much information on you as possible, and in others we will use narrative elements to show you how this stuff can work in the real world.

Why is all this tax stuff so important?

People tend to think about taxes only a few times per year. Most people have their taxes withheld from their paychecks, and they feel like they get a little bonus every year when they file (if they get a refund). Even if someone employed all the strategies outlined in this book and saved thousands of dollars, they wouldn't see that money until they filed their tax return. On the other hand, we bet if there were an immediate reward, like if a little tax man followed you around and said, "Hey – if you put that receipt in this envelope instead of the trash I'll give you twenty dollars." Or, "Psst, if you send these emails before you book your trip I can give you a 35% discount off your flights and hotel," then everyone would minimize their tax bill to the smallest extent possible.

Unfortunately, it doesn't work that way, but the strategies we have outlined in this book do work. If you use them correctly, you *will* save money. "Saving money" sounds boring, doesn't it? It sure sounds less sexy than earning money. So let's re-frame our thoughts about taxes, at least until you put down this book. Want to earn some extra cash you can use to fund your next family vacation? How about earning a bonus you can use to pay down your house or redecorate the living room? This book, and all this stuff about taxes, will help you earn that bonus, if you're willing to do a tiny amount of work for it. In fact, we've done some math to make sure the strategies we're proposing will be worth your time to implement – we wouldn't recommend you spend twenty hours to save five dollars, dig?

Why is all this tax stuff so important for businesses?

Any business is only as valuable as the cash it generates. It's a concept as old as time, and it's true no matter what "new" economy we happen to be in. Someone might say, "No way, Amazon is worth billions and it operates at a loss." Yes, but it is worth billions because people can look into the future and see that eventually it will generate piles and piles of profit. "But some businesses are valued on clicks." Yes, because savvy business people can figure out how to turn clicks into cash, even if it's not readily apparent at this very moment.

If a business is as valuable as the cash it generates (or will generate, of course), then a business is more valuable if it generates more cash, right? Right.

Now imagine you have a business, and you have a partner. Your partner is silent, meaning they don't do anything or even offer any useful advice. You can't buy this partner out, and they don't offer any investment in your company. In fact, sometimes it seems like all they really do is tell you what you *can't* do, and sometimes it seems like it takes forever to get them to give you permission to do anything. We think you will agree this doesn't sound like the most desirable partner, but there is a big saving grace: Your partner is the one who makes the rules about how much you have to pay him. How is that a saving grace, you ask? Well, if they makes the rules, you don't have to feel bad about using those rules to pay them as little as possible.

We're sure you easily figured out that the partner in the above scenario is the government. Before anyone gets annoyed with us, yes, we agree the government does many wonderful things, and we love the roads, the police, the schools, the firefighters, and the other things the government provides, it's just that it's not always a great business partner. We believe that there's nothing immoral about using the government's laws to pay what is owed, and no more.

There is another, more tangible reason to minimize taxes: Remember when we said that a business is valued based on how much cash it generates? Well, cash that doesn't go to taxes increases the value of the business. Saving taxes means you have a business that pays you and your employees more. It means you can re-invest and grow your business more easily. And it's possible that certain businesses that aren't profitable might be, if we can just figure out how to make their tax liability work. In other words, saving taxes can keep your business running even in tough times, and it can change your operating metrics in such a way that you can make your idea a money maker instead of a money loser.

Disclaimer

What tax book would be complete without a disclaimer? We bet you can already guess what our disclaimer is going to be, but just in case, here it is: Tax laws change all the time, sometimes in big ways, and sometimes in very small ways, and sometimes there are expiration dates built into the laws. Tax laws are incredibly complex, and we have simplified things here and there in order to avoid the confusion that the tax code tends to engender. We have carefully chosen topics and stories based on principles that aren't likely to change much, but you can bet your last dollar that *something* with respect to the tax law for each chapter will change by the time you read this book. Again: the best way to use this book is as a conversation starter with your tax professional or your business consultant. It is not meant to be a substitute for sound, timely advice. We will discuss in great detail how to go about choosing your tax pro a little later on in the book.

Michael A. York, EA
Andrew L. Stevens, EA, MBA

The IRS is not the enemy

Who doesn't live in fear of a letter from the IRS? You grab the mail, chuck the junk in the garbage, and sitting there in a white envelope is some mystery communique marked "IRS." You have the feeling of being gut-punched, where you can't tell if you want to rip it open to read the bad news or if you never want to open it at all.

What if we told you that the IRS is nothing to be afraid of? What if we made the outrageous claim that the IRS is not your enemy (in the same way that if you're not an international drug smuggler, the DEA isn't your enemy, either)? We all file tax returns, and we all do our best to make sure we follow the law while also keeping our fair share of the money we earn, right? The fear comes from the idea that we might make a simple mistake that, after years of accrued penalties and interest, will cost us our homes and our retirement accounts in one instant. Imagine finding out you've gone through an expensive divorce and you didn't even know you were married.

Let's talk realistically about the IRS. Yes, they audit people. Yes, in those audits they try to determine if the person has followed the law and has been honest about how they have reported income and expenses. Yes, sometimes they disagree with people about what is fair and what is legal. But the truth is: the IRS doesn't have the final say in *any* of these things.

Tax laws are written and passed by Congress, not by the Internal Revenue Service. In its role of tax enforcement, the IRS interprets those laws and writes guidelines to aid the general public when preparing tax returns and to aid its agents when reviewing those same tax returns. These guidelines are necessary because what comes out of Congress can be pretty ambiguous and unclear (big surprise, right?).

Here's an example that pertains to S-Corporations, which is a business entity that could potentially benefit a lot of people reading this book (talk to your tax professional). As far as we can tell there is no single law passed by Congress that describes how S-Corp officers should be paid. Instead, there are a bunch of revenue rulings and tax court cases that have given us information we have to interpret and apply on a case-by-case basis. The IRS has done the work of collecting and collating all of these rulings and tax court outcomes and provided guidance that we use to determine what's fair. However, the reason these rulings keep piling up is that often people disagree with the IRS, and sometimes the court says the IRS is right, and sometimes they say the taxpayer is right. Thus, even if the IRS has a guideline, that doesn't mean it's the end-all-be-all. For the purpose of this book, we're going to stick with the IRS guidelines just to be safe, but if you strongly believe you are right, you can always challenge the IRS in tax court, and you just might win.

The IRS interprets the law and all of the court cases and provides guidance for taxpayers, but of course the main thing they're known for is enforcing those laws. Enforcement is surely where the scary part comes in, right? Well, we would argue that if you a) have a good tax professional on your side, b) are fair and honest with how you provide your information to that tax professional, and c) run your business in a professional manner with professional records, then you have very little to worry about. Here's the best part: A lot of the laws and guidelines on the books can greatly benefit you if you know about them. Congress is constantly passing tax laws to goose the economy or provide relief for certain types of taxpayers, and you can take advantage of those laws.

Congress may have an idea of a certain type of taxpayer they want to help, and if we're being cynical we might presume that it is a taxpayer who just made a huge campaign contribution. Let's call him Carl. But here's the thing: they can't simply write a law that says, "If you are the certain Carl who just gave us all that money you get to take advantage of these deductions." Instead they have to describe Carl in loose terms, and that leads us to the good part: If you can be described in the same terms as Carl, or if you can *make* yourself more like Carl, you can take advantage of the same deductions as Carl. Your tax professional's job is to help you figure out all the ways you can strategize to benefit from the "work" Carl has done, and the IRS's job is not to shout, "Hey, you're not Carl!" Instead, the IRS's job is to simply verify that you do, in fact, look enough like Carl.

> ### *Don't Go There Doug!*
> Doug knows just how to handle an audit! In fact, he saw this strategy work in a movie once. He thinks that when the IRS auditor asks for a receipt, he will simply dump a mountain of papers onto the table and say, "It's in there – find it!" Then Doug will laugh and laugh as the auditor searches through the mountain of receipts, before finally quitting in frustration. Don't go there, Doug! Audits don't work like that! In fact, it's up to the taxpayer to provide documentation in order to justify deductions. You give them exactly what they ask for, when they ask for it. IRS examiners are careful professionals, and treating them any other way isn't going to help your case if you want to have a "no change" audit.

Why are we talking about this? We want to drive home an important point about your business: You should be eager to report income to the IRS. Reporting income from your business is what allows you to strategize your taxes to save even more money by morphing your business to look like the specific "Carl" that is most advantageous, and you also get closer to helpful "safe harbors" the IRS uses to classify businesses and hobbies. We all know that person who is paranoid about the IRS finding out about income, and you don't have to be that person. Instead, if you do things the right way you can sleep well at night *and* get a bunch of great (and perfectly legal) tax deductions.

Just remember this: The IRS is not your enemy; they simply interpret and enforce the laws passed by Congress. Because those laws are often confusing and ambiguous, the IRS has issued guidelines and provided "safe harbors." A tax break available to some is available to all, and you should be eager to report income because it opens up additional tax strategies. Finally, if you follow your tax professional's advice, letters from the IRS won't cause the extreme anxiety they once did.

Eve the artist

Key topics in this story:
Tax
- When is it ethical to claim you have a business?
- Claiming deductions before you have made a profit.
- Financial "cushion" before profits are realized.
- Profit motive.

Tax savings potential: $$$$$

We have changed the names of pretty much everyone in this book, except for Eve. The reason is a good one: she's the mother of one of the authors. Eve has had a lot of different careers, hobbies, and passions, and she has been successful with pretty much all of them, although they didn't all make money. For example, her years in the real estate business were much more lucrative than her hobby of collecting ukuleles, though she was great at both.

Eve has always been very right-brain oriented. She is a writer, she plays the piano and the ukulele, and she is a phenomenal cook. About ten years ago Eve decided she would like to learn more about fine art. Specifically, she wanted to learn how to paint. Her mother was a well-known artist and painter; in fact, she was so talented that it was a little discouraging to other people in the family who wanted to explore art, because their work might be the subject of an unfavorable comparison. Still, Eve pressed on, and she began taking art classes, starting with basic sketching, watercolor, figure drawing, and so on.

A brief aside: Very frequently when we talk to a client about the idea of starting a business, we hear a response like, "I've heard this idea before - you want me to create a business so I can open up potential tax deductions or 'scam' the government and say I have a business when I haven't made any money." Honest people worry that deducting expenses before a profit is made is against the rules or is unethical. Eve's story is to help you understand that there is nothing illegal or unethical about taking business tax deductions, when

Michael A. York, EA
Andrew L. Stevens, EA, MBA

done correctly. In fact, most businesses incur substantial costs well before any revenue is earned, and art is a great example of that kind of business (for another example see "Pete" a little later on). If you have a true profit motive there is a great chance that you will make a profit eventually, and when you do, the IRS will not have mixed feelings about taking their cut. You shouldn't feel bad for taking a justifiable deduction in the meantime.

Back to our story: At this early stage Eve didn't have a profit motive; she was simply learning the skills of being an artist. Over the years her talent began to emerge, and she was accepted into a prestigious art program. We want to stress that none of this happened overnight, and there wasn't some moment where Eve and the rest of the world suddenly realized that she is a genius artist. Eve worked and worked at painting, and she incurred plenty of expenses along the way as she developed her talent.

After years of work, Eve and a friend co-signed on a lease for an art studio they share that is part of a big gallery complex. Eve's lease stipulated that she would hang some of her work in the gallery area so patrons could have a chance to see and purchase the art.

It only took about three months until all of Eve's paintings in the gallery had sold. Next, all of the finished pieces in the studio sold, too. After that, all of the unfinished pieces sold, even those with wet paint on the canvas. She even took commissions for paintings, which means she sold art she hadn't even created yet. As of the moment we're writing this, Andy's mother is in New York to visit museums and explore her artistic inspiration, and just before the trip she sold a small painting for enough money to pay for two tickets to *Hamilton*. *Hamilton*! Maybe by the time you're reading this, *Hamilton* tickets will be free, but right now they're really, really expensive. She took a few bucks worth of oil paint, a canvas, and some brushes, and through some alchemy we don't understand (because it took years to develop and cost plenty of money), she turned them into *Hamilton* tickets in a few hours.

> ### *Don't Go There Doug!*
> Doug wants to be a professional artist, so he says, "I declare myself officially to be in business!" Doug enrolls in the local university to take his first art classes, and he books a trip to Spain to learn from Picasso's dog walker's neighbor, where he learns to doodle on old refrigerator boxes. Don't go there, Doug! Education expenses to learn a new career aren't deductible as business expenses! Only once you're in business is "continuing education" deductible. With a brand new business, you can't use your training and education as business expenses.

Now you might be thinking, "This story doesn't apply to me at all. I'm not artistic, I don't have artist's genes, and I'm not going to sell any art." Well, Andy's mom doesn't have artist's genes either (she was adopted). She also didn't consider herself an artist before she got into painting, believe it or not, and when she began to study art she certainly didn't think she would make money as an artist (she's not crazy, after all). So how does this apply to you? Well, do you think if you spent ten years working diligently to purse a passion or hobby, you might get good enough at it to make some money, especially if you followed the IRS's guidelines about establishing and following a profit motive? We think you could! Depending on what you pursue, it might not even take ten years.

> ### *Hot Tax Tip*
> The IRS guidelines about what constitutes a business (versus a hobby) are actually a pretty great blueprint for how to start a profitable business!

Michael A. York, EA
Andrew L. Stevens, EA, MBA

If we agree that you could make money doing something you're passionate about, then when is it ethical to take tax deductions for the cash you put into the endeavor? If it's only ethical to do so once you're making money, then you might end up with a business like Eve's, where products sell for big bucks, but your cost of goods sold includes paint (basically free), canvas (basically free), paint brushes (not free, but they get reused a lot), and framing (not free, but you don't always have to frame the piece). But is that all that Eve's customers are paying for? Paint, canvas, and framing? Or is the cost of the art*work* (see, work is right there in the name) something else entirely?

Let's look a little deeper into the idea of deducting expenses before a profit is actually made. The IRS is happy to collect tax on all of the juicy profit when Eve sells a painting, but as we discussed, isn't the customer really paying for the talent of the artist? Was that talent developed overnight, and was it developed for free? The answer to both of those questions is no! Thus, expenses incurred to develop the artist's talent (and provide inspiration) are legitimate business expenses, even if they occurred well before the artist made any money. These expenses might be deductible in the year incurred, they might be additional training (sometimes deductible, sometimes not), or they might even be amortizable start-up costs. The important point is that they help provide the financial cushion that many need in order to get their businesses from pre-revenue to profitability, and that's part of what Congress intended when they wrote these tax code provisions into law.

Still, we have clients who worry, "I've heard this idea before: you want me to 'scam' the government and say I have a business when I haven't made any money!" Again: *We would never scam the government!* We believe in following the law as written by Congress and as interpreted by the IRS. Deducting expenses before a profit is made is not against the rules if you have a legitimate profit motive, you run your business like any other legitimate business, and pay your fair share of taxes once you do start making money. In other words, it's not wrong if you literally do everything by the book, which is what we help people do. So, when should you (or Eve or anyone) start taking deductions? The answer is: the moment you decide to pursue a profit and are ready to conduct yourself accordingly. That's it!

Whether you already have made a profit or won't have one for several years, as long as you have a true profit motive and run your business like a real business, you can be assured of two things: First, you're not doing anything unusual or unethical. Second, the IRS will be happy to take its cut once the cash starts rolling in. The only thing preventing you from declaring yourself to be in business is a change in attitude toward profit motive, an idea for something you can put some effort behind, and the discipline to keep timely, accurate records.

> **Questions for your tax professional:**
> 1. How can I tell if I have a business or a hobby?
> 2. How do the IRS guidelines on profit motive apply to my business?
> 3. When are education and training deductible as a business expense?

Pete and every restaurant, ever

Key topics in this story:
Tax

- Hobby vs. Business.
- Start-up costs.
- Deducting losses before a profit is realized.

Tax savings potential: $$$$$

Maybe you're not convinced by Eve's story because you've heard the line that the IRS will consider your business a "hobby" until you make a profit. Maybe your tax professional has even told you point-blank that anything that doesn't earn a profit is a hobby. We're going to try one more time to convince you by telling you about a very common business that we're all familiar with: The typical restaurant.

There could be a restaurant out there that was profitable from day one, but we've never heard of it. In real life, every restaurant, whether it's a food truck or a popup or a diner or a Michelin-starred fine dining establishment, incurs lots of expenses long before they ever earn a profit, and no one considers them a hobby.

Let's talk about our friend Pete, a chef who opened a restaurant. We'll skip most of Pete's backstory and just tell you he always dreamed of opening his own restaurant. Like all aspiring restaurateurs, he figured he could bootstrap the business. He'd begin by selling his food out of his home, then when he made enough money he would rent a small space, and when he made more money he would buy tables and chairs and ovens and ranges and pots and pans and dishes, and when he made even more money he would hire staff. He figured he could pay for all of those expenses out of the profits he made along the way. Wait, that's impossible: no customer is going to spend money at a restaurant that doesn't have tables and chairs and staff and a kitchen. In real life, Pete incurred plenty of start-up and "organizational" costs (costs that have to be incurred before the business can open, like permitting and lawyer's fees) and he paid out the nose for equipment and furnishings and rent before his restaurant opened.

Don't Go There Doug!
Doug wants to sell homemade beet pie out of a food truck that doubles as a party catering business and is also the worst ride-share vehicle, ever. He claims to use his home kitchen as his "home office," because he makes most of the components of his beet pies there. Don't go there, Doug! Home offices need to be used "regularly and exclusively" for business, and while a kitchen might be used regularly, it's tough to argue it's used exclusively for business unless there is a second kitchen in the home used for personal meal preparation.

Even after he started taking reservations, it took a while for Pete's restaurant to catch on. During those first few months Pete earned a little revenue here and there, but his expenses, including staff, linen service, produce purveyors, and more added up to huge losses. When Pete's restaurant was operating at a loss, do you think anyone dared claim that his food cost wasn't a legitimate business expense? Would anyone say with a straight face that Pete was indulging in a hobby from Day One until his revenue was greater than his expenses?

Not only are Pete's early losses deductible, they're part of what enables him to be in business in the first place. The ability to recoup some of those losses in the form of tax deductions (including capital loss carryforwards) is part of the calculus that every business undertakes when planning out finances and capital requirements. It's normal, and virtually every business does it!

So how did Pete's restaurant make out? Most new restaurants don't survive, and Pete nearly closed his doors on a few occasions. In fact, if not for the tax savings that his early losses generated, he would have surely closed. After five years in business, however, Pete's restaurant is doing well, and he's about to open another location. This expansion will surely incur plenty of upfront costs and generate plenty of losses long before it ever becomes profitable, but these are all legitimate business expenses.

Questions for your tax professional:
1. Do I need to earn a profit in order to deduct my expenses?
2. What does it mean to deduct expenses anyway?

Michael A. York, EA
Andrew L. Stevens, EA, MBA

Section Two: Why and how to start a business

Why start a business in the first place?

If we haven't said it yet, we'll say it again and again and again in the coming pages: tax laws are lobbied for and written by influential people who want an advantage. The vast majority of those people own businesses, and they want to get a tax break for their businesses. The government also often believes that the best way to goose the economy is by stimulating small businesses, and they tend to do that through the tax code. Thus, if you have a business, you can take advantage of the tax laws to save money. These are not loopholes, but the laws put in place quite intentionally. There are great reasons for starting a business other than saving money on taxes, but it could be a big consideration.

> <u>Business Tip</u>
> Having a small business that you run will likely give you opportunities to practice skills that will make you better at your full-time job!

If you have a regular W2 job and you start a new business, it will probably make you a better employee at your original job (as long as it doesn't distract you from your regular duties). How? Many employees fall into a rut where they take their jobs for granted, and running a business with a real profit motive will illustrate, in vivid detail, the tightrope most businesses walk between profit and loss. It will also give you extra opportunities to practice negotiation, public speaking, pricing, marketing, business modeling, sales, and a host of other activities that probably fall outside of your regular duties. Think about this scenario: You work a normal job, and you never have opportunities to speak to suppliers, call on customers, or give presentations. However, you run a business on the side where you do those things frequently. Then one day your boss is stuck in Dayton when they're supposed to give a presentation to a group of corporate partners, and because you've been "practicing" these skills with your own business, you have the confidence to step up and nail it. That might sound like an unlikely scenario, but running your own business will give you enhanced abilities, and the confidence to act if necessary. Are we talking about business superpowers, perhaps? Yes we are!

If your business takes off, the main benefit is the extra financial security. Imagine being in a situation where you have ownership of this thing that requires some work on your days off, but it pays you cash outside of your regular wages. That financial benefit might help you and your family through an emergency, and it might even be something you can pass down to your children to enhance their financial positions. Oh yeah, if you're one of the lucky ones you might even be able to quit your job and focus full time on your business. Even if you don't quit your job, you will likely retire someday. When you retire from your regular job, you don't get to sell your job to the next person. However, you can sell your small business if you no longer wish to run it, and thus "quitting" your business could actually put a lump of cash in your bank account.

Finally, our experience has shown that if you put some of the strategies outlined in this book to work this year and find a good tax professional, you could save hundreds (if not thousands) of dollars when you file your return. But here's the thing: most tax deduction strategies can be repeated every year, so not only will you save big bucks this year, you will save it next year as well. And the year after. If you keep at it, you might be able to keep saving every year for the rest of your life. Seriously!

Types of small businesses

The businesses referenced in this book are, by nature, small businesses. A "small" business isn't defined by how much money it earns, how many people it employs, how many states or countries it makes sales in, how long it has been in business, or even how many shareholders there are. The most important distinction is really one of complexity. I'll give you an example: Once upon a time, someone had to conceive of the idea of overnight shipping and all the logistical details that go into it. That kind of business was never a "small" business, even on their first day, because the amount of complexity involved in terms of raising capital, attaining economies of scale, negotiating inter-state commerce laws, contracting with suppliers, raising awareness among consumers (and making sales) and executing their operations in a profitable manner means that they needed to exist as a big business, or not at all.

> <u>Business Tip</u>
> A small business just means it's a relatively simple business, but plenty of small businesses make piles and piles of cash.

Another example of a business that is never a "small" business is a medical device start-up. From day one, a new medical device requires an incredible amount of teamwork and investment to make it to market. Consider how the users (doctors and nurses) are different from the buyers (hospitals and clinics) who are different from the payers (insurance companies) who are different from the people the product is used for (patients). That's a lot of stakeholders to make happy! And you only get to that point once the biggest stakeholder of them all (the federal government in the form of the FDA) is satisfied. Even if they have zero revenue for years, a medical device start-up is by necessity a "bigger" business than someone who sells products on Amazon, even though that person might make a tremendous amount of money.

Why is this book just about small businesses? Well, for starters, we've said many times that big businesses have a lot of different in-house specialties, like marketing, sales, finance, and so on. One of those in-house specialties is tax, and those tax specialists are very good at mining the tax code. We think everyone should pay their fair share, and we also think that small business owners should have a chance to ethically reduce their tax bill, too. Another reason we have focused solely on small businesses is that we find that many small business owners have a proclivity toward wanting to do things on their own, and we would like to reach them with a simple idea: It's a good idea to hire experts when you can. No one can be an expert in all things, and in many cases it can be distracting to focus on things that aren't the core matters that make money for your business. Check out "Beth and the One Function You Should Always Outsource" for a great example of a business function you should probably hire out. If you're convinced and you're open to hiring out a second function, might we suggest tax planning and preparation?

A few types of small businesses

A question we're often asked is, "I want to start a business, but I don't have any good ideas." If that's the case, our first suggestion is that you might be thinking too broadly, and it will help to organize how you think about businesses in order to "mine" your experience and passion. Plus, believe it or not, getting granular will help focus your thinking and may help you realize you actually DO have an idea for a business, maybe even lots of ideas for businesses. We will give you an example: If we were to ask you, "Hey, I'm thinking about moving for work, do you know anyone who can help me?" That is such a broad question, with so many variables, that most people would just say, "No." But if we said, "Hey, I'm thinking about moving to New York to work in financial services. Do you know anyone who has lived in New York that I could talk to? Or do you know anyone who has worked in finance before?" We bet you can think of at least one or two people who fit that narrow description. Asking a specific question rather than a broad one helped you come up with a helpful answer. Coming up with ideas for businesses works the same way.

Side hustles

A side hustle is a business that you run in addition to your regular full-time job. By definition, it's a lower priority than your full-time gig, but that doesn't make it something you're doing for "fun." Even if it takes less of your time by necessity, and you tend to focus on it during your off hours, you're still working hard, taking care of customers, and aiming for big profits.

Determining a good idea for a side hustle can be tricky. The idea is to keep it to something that won't consume your every waking hour. Running a brick and mortar establishment is probably out, as is something where you will have to supervise employees as they do their work.

To determine an idea for a side hustle, start by taking inventory of your current job. What are all of your roles and responsibilities, and what are the tools of your trade? Once you have this list in hand, go through it line by line, and look for opportunities to create products or services that you can sell. We'll give you some examples.

Michael A. York, EA
Andrew L. Stevens, EA, MBA

Luis worked as a manager at a big specialty hardwood retailer. As manager, he was responsible for supervising employees, managing customer service issues, tracking inventory and ordering replenishments of hardwoods, and doing the same for the limited number of tools and supplies they carried. Customers often asked about tools they didn't stock, things like vintage planes, spokeshaves, scrapers, chisels, gouges, and so on. Why did they want vintage tools? Well, once upon a time those tools were made in the USA out of top-quality steel, and they were built to last. New examples of those tools are still made, but they are very expensive, often commanding prices ten to twenty times more than the common tools made abroad and sold in home improvement stores. Luis had an idea: He had seen some old rusted planes and other tools at garage sales, but he never thought much of it. Often they were being given away for a few bucks. However, Luis knew that with a little TLC, a little sharpening and polishing, and maybe a new handle here and there, those old tools could be made brand new again, and sold on eBay for a huge markup. Luis's side hustle was born: On weekends, he and wife would go to estate sales and garage sales to look for antiques, which she loved. While she browsed old furniture, he would grab any old hand tools he could find. With a little work, his eBay store was in business, earning between $50 to $150 in profit per sale. After a few months he was well-known to the people who run estate sales in his city, and they would call him first with any hand tools they wanted to unload. Then one day a big call came in – a long time estate sale consultant was moving his storage to a new location, and rather than box up a bunch of heavy tools, he called Luis to see if he would take them. When all was said and done Luis paid $500 for inventory that he turned into $25,000 in sales from that one transaction alone.

To recap: through his regular job, Luis was able to identify a market that he thought he might be able to serve. By networking with local people, he was able to find great deals on inventory, and with a little work he flipped that inventory for a very tidy profit. Prior to starting this business, if someone were to ask him, "Luis, do you have an idea for a small business?" he would have said no. However, by opening himself up to the opportunities presented by the "insider" knowledge he gained from his regular job, he was able to carve out a nice little side hustle.

One more example: Jane worked as a residential real estate agent, and her husband worked in finance. Jane's clients were constantly getting rid of perfectly good pieces of furniture that didn't work in their new homes. Jane and her husband were able to pick up a few pieces of furniture for their house for very cheap, and Jane remarked to her husband that their house looked better after replacing a few pieces here and there. However, soon they began turning down all the pieces her clients offered because they didn't have room. That's when Jane had an idea. She and her husband rented a storage unit and began filling it with the odd armoires, beds, throw pillows, and breakfast tables her clients couldn't take with them. When they felt like they had accumulated enough pieces they began a staging business. When someone scheduled an open house for an empty home, Jane would hire some local movers to haul furniture from her storage unit to the house and leave it there until the place sold. For a few hundred dollars a month for the storage unit and another couple of hundred dollars for the movers she was able to charge $1000 to $3000 per house. And the best part – these weren't even her clients, so it was a great way to meet new people and make money from other agent's listings.

To recap, Jane seized on an opportunity that she discovered via her regular job – one that required very little investment, and even less time to manage.

Passion projects

Passion projects are businesses where the chief goal isn't making money. There can be great financial benefits that we will discuss later, and there is surely a profit motive, but the main reason for pursuing the business is something else. Toms Shoes is a great example of a passion project. The founder was traveling abroad and noticed how many impoverished children lacked shoes. He set about to found a company that would be able to provide free shoes to children around the world and make money doing it. Since then, they have expanded into other markets like coffee, eyewear, apparel, etc., and each product has a philanthropic goal above and beyond bottom line profit. Whether the founder knew the company would be a massive success is beside the point: he started it because he was passionate about helping children.

Passion projects don't have to be about helping people in a tangible way, they just have to be something you're passionate about. There is often overlap between passion projects and former hobbies, but the key difference is that a hobby is something you do to pass the time, to keep your mind occupied, to relieve boredom, maybe to connect with other people. A passion project is something you obsess over. It's something you don't just do to fill up your waking hours, it's something you would make time for no matter what. We know a very successful inventor who has patented a ton of devices, has started, run, and sold businesses, has a family, and manages an impressive portfolio of investments and royalty streams. Yet, he is obsessed with magic and makes time to work on it every day. At any time, he has at least three decks of cards with him. If your kids get near him at a party, they will be delighted by a magic show that would rival anything in Las Vegas. He's been known to skip out of technology conferences where he is the key presenter in order to meet up with another magician to share notes and show each other tricks. He recently started a podcast to preserve the conversations he has with fellow magicians and the knowledge he gains, and to share it with other aspiring magicians (no, they don't discuss how tricks are done). The podcast has a small following and it is beginning to pick up some advertisers here and there, and one day it may be a very profitable endeavor. There is surely a profit motive for his podcast, but the inventor would still be involved in magic regardless of whether his podcast business is a success.

One more: A successful attorney we know is passionate about helping people learn to live better lives through a firm moral and ethical code. We know, we know, it's an oxymoron for an attorney to be passionate about ethics, but this one claims to be. He and a writing partner spend a lot of time talking to people who actually have strong personal ethics, and they compile these stories into books, which they self-publish on Amazon. Do they make money? Maybe a tiny amount, but the real "profit" comes from improving their own ethical codes (and believe me, as attorneys they need all the help they can get!). The books also help them market themselves to new clients, and help reassure existing clients that they have found ethical representation. As a passion project this is a good one; while the sales of the books aren't going to send anyone's kids to college, the extra benefits from enhancing the writers' personal brands are very lucrative, indeed.

Home run swings

A home run swing is a business that could have a huge payoff, but the chances of success are small. Fortunately, you can get great tax benefits even if your business never makes money, and we will talk about that in another section.

While you read these examples of home run swing-style businesses, just keep in mind that the critical thing is running the business in a professional manner and having a legitimate profit motive.

The most famous "home run swing" example we can think of is a man who decided to become a professional golfer. We all know that the best way to get better at golf is to go back in time and start playing at a younger age, but his man decided to go about it another way. He took lessons, practiced, played a lot, and participated in tournaments. If that sounds like almost every golfer you know, we're not surprised. What this man did differently was run his golfing "business" just like any other business: he tracked his expenses very carefully, he created an entity for the business, he took advantage of opportunities to earn revenue, he changed his business model from time-to-time to try to become profitable, and when he entered a tournament he kept his total expenses below the prize money for finishing in first place. Unlike everyone else who plays golf for fun, this man demonstrated a level of professionalism and a profit motive, and when the IRS audited him and later took him to court, he prevailed. Now, if he had actually become a professional golfer he would have been able to potentially make a great deal of money, but obviously the chances of that happening were quite slim, hence why we consider this business a "home run swing."

A better example comes from people who develop smartphone apps and games in their spare time. It might be impossible to know what the next app like Whatsapp or Angry Birds will be, but if you are the one to develop it you are set for life. In the meantime, you will incur expenses and likely have very little revenue, and thus you will operate at a loss for several years. That's ok, as long as you follow the rules we'll talk about elsewhere in the "safe harbors" section.

Former hobbies

A hobby is a great way to learn a skill, meet people and develop a network, collect tools and equipment, and get to know the ins and outs of something without taking much risk. A hobby, however, is not a business. The IRS has very clear guidelines on what constitutes a hobby versus a business, and we will expound on that in another section. For now, just understand that there are definite distinctions, and this book is not about how to simply use your existing hobby to deduct a bunch of stuff. However, after spending years in a hobby, there is a decent chance that you have amassed enough expertise to go a step further and undertake the additional effort to start a business. "Eve the Artist" is a great example of a business that started out as a hobby.

> ### Business Tip
> A hobby is not a business, but some of the best ideas for businesses come from former hobbies.

If you're already engaged in something that you can make profitable with a little extra effort, it should make it easy to come up with an idea for a business. How about an example?

> ### Don't Go There Doug!
> Doug has collected plastic building blocks since he was a kid, and he wants to deduct all of his past purchases as business expenses, claiming his home is now a museum for all of his toys. He hasn't done any advertising or even invited anyone over to look his models, and they're not even for sale! He also wants to go to the plastic building block amusement park and see the movies based on building block characters and take a "business" deduction. Don't go there, Doug! If you don't have a true profit motive, and you don't act like a business, you're not in business.

Jesse's hobby was pistol marksmanship. He participated at small local competitions almost every weekend, and a few times per year he traveled to national competitions. He participated in this hobby for several years, occasionally winning small prizes here and there. When it came to starting a business, he didn't have to think very hard about what to do. Through years of practice, he had developed the expertise to go into business giving marksmanship lessons to new shooters. The hobby itself was never going to be a profitable business: the prizes at matches never amounted to more than he spent on travel, training, and supplies. However, by marketing his expertise, he was able to make a profit teaching people the skills he had developed. Without his hobby, he wouldn't have devoted the time and resources to cultivating his skills. Once he had, he realized that he actually had something marketable to sell.

It's important to note that Jesse didn't simply claim that his hobby was suddenly a business. His hobby wasn't a business, and he didn't run it that way. However, he was able to develop marketable expertise and figure out a way to profit from it, and that aspect allowed him to build a business around it.

One more example: Hanna grew up in Hartford speaking Hungarian at home with her parents and older brother, and she studied Spanish in school. She met and married an Argentinian man, and they lived in Buenos Aires for seven years before moving back to the US. While in Argentina, she enjoyed the Spanish immersion and became fluent much faster than she expected she would. She realized that she had a knack for picking up languages (more like a superpower!), and she began using any resource available to learn Italian, Polish, French, and German. By the time she got back to the states she was fluent in everything but Polish, though she could carry on a decent conversation. Her friends were always fascinated by her abilities, and often asked about tips for materials, courses, and techniques for learning new languages. She started a group email chain to share her knowledge, and that became a blog, and that became a rich online community of language learners around the world. That community features advertisements, and advertisements provide revenue, and that revenue allowed Hanna to take a piece of her hobby and turn it into a profitable business.

Now: let's meet some real people, see how they started their businesses, and learn how they used some amazing tax strategies to keep more of their hard-earned money.

Michael A. York, EA
Andrew L. Stevens, EA, MBA

Section Three - Real Stories of Tax & Business Strategies

Tax Planner Brianne

Tax savings potential: $$$$

Key topics in this story:
Tax
- Why schedule a tax planning meeting?
- How does tax planning work?

Imagine an alternate reality where, just before you die, you can get a list of all the things you need to do in order to get into heaven. Would you want that list, or would you gamble that you've lived a sufficiently pious life? Now imagine that just before the year ends, you can get a list of everything you need to do in order to save money on taxes. Would you want that list in time to act, or would you celebrate the new year and hope you don't have to pay too much when you file? The tax year for just about everyone ends on December 31 at midnight, and as we scream "Happy New Year!" the previous tax year ends and changes that can be made to it are limited.

Our friend Brianne used to think that if she got great tax advice at the beginning of the year, she could govern herself appropriately, run her business well, and end up paying her (minimum) fair share of taxes. She was correct to a degree, but planning taxes is sort of like making chili: a lot goes into it, it's easy to mess up, and some tweaks are often required along the way. Tax advice at the beginning of the year is like a recipe: it tells you what to do in general terms, but it doesn't tell you whether the finished product is correct or not. Tax planning at the end of the year is like tasting the chili before you serve it: you can adjust the finished product in a way that ends up making all the difference. If you're going to make chili, it's nice to have a great recipe AND taste the chili to see if it needs more spice or more salt; likewise, it's great to be able to utilize professional tax advice throughout the year. It's even better if you can make adjustments at the end based on your actual results.

So how does tax planning work, exactly? In Brianne's case, she runs her business as usual during the year, and calls up her friendly tax planners when she has a tax question. At the end of the year she gathers up as much documentation as possible and brings it in to an appointment. We construct a rough version of her tax return and look for ways she can save money before the clock strikes midnight on December 31. We work with Brianne to make sure any tax strategies she employs will also work with her business strategy, and at the end we re-run her rough tax return to figure out how much she will save by making a few adjustments.

What are those adjustments? A lot of the basic ideas are peppered throughout this book, but the key is they're tailored to the individual client, like Brianne. Sometimes we advise she accelerates some purchases she was planning to save for a future year, and sometimes we recommend she delays on some things she was planning to do right away.

Here's a great example: One holiday season, Brianne was planning to give all of her employees $50 gift cards as Christmas gifts in addition to their year-end bonuses. She didn't realize that she would have to include that $50 as employee wages, which meant that she would have to pay the company's share of FICA and other payroll taxes in addition to the $50. In other words, her gift cards would end up costing her more than $50 each, and her employees would receive less than $50, because they get taxed on the value of the gift card. (Wait, what kind of system makes it cost more than $50 to give someone less than $50? The American Tax Code!).

We helped Brianne figure out how to plan a holiday party for her employees where all the expenses of the party would be fully deductible (including food and drinks), and where she could give out actual gifts to each employee and their families and get a tax deduction for the price she paid for the gifts. Oh yeah: by giving actual gifts rather than gift cards, Brianne got a tax deduction, but the price of the gift wasn't taxable to the employee. Was this a huge tax savings? No, but the savings from just this one idea paid for her tax planning appointment, and every other recommendation she received was icing on the cake.

Circa 2008, we recommended that Brianne buy a piece of equipment she had scheduled to purchase the following year. She said, "If I save tax this year by buying this stuff, doesn't that mean I won't get the tax savings next year, and thus it's all the same?" She had a point, but in our opinion it's better to get a tax savings now rather than plan to get one later. The next year the recession hit, and Brianne's business struggled. She ended up with a loss the following year, so the tax benefit from buying the equipment would have been zero. By buying the equipment when we recommended it, Brianne got a nice tax break and the savings came at a time when her business was struggling with cash flow.

Once the clock strikes midnight on December 31 there is very little that anyone can do to change their income and expenses for the previous year. That's why we recommend that most people (in our practices it's pretty much mandatory if you have a business) meet with a good tax planner in November or December to get a sense of how much tax they are going to end up paying, and how they can minimize that number.

Don't Go There Doug!
Doug hasn't kept any records of expenses, doesn't have a sense of how much money his business has made, and he still wants to sit down to find out the exact amount he will need to withdraw from his grandmother's bank account to pay his taxes. Being Doug, he schedules his appointment for December 31. Don't go there, Doug! We can always generalize some strategies to save, but we need precise numbers if you want precise advice. Make sure you visit your tax professional early enough to take action on the advice you receive!

Questions for your tax professional:
1. Do you offer year-end tax planning? If so, when do you prefer your clients to schedule such appointments?
2. What documents should I bring to my tax planning appointment?

Give contributions as advertising rather than donations

Tax savings potential: $$$

Key topics in this story:
Tax
- How to get the most benefit for your business for charitable activities.
- Charitable donations and self-employment tax.
- How the Tax Cuts & Jobs Act makes business donations irrelevant for many people.
- How businesses calculate the real benefit of making charitable donations.

If you've ever owned, run, or even just answered the phones at a business, you know you get hit up for charitable contributions with some frequency. Sometimes it's the local junior high asking if you can donate something for the softball team's fundraiser, sometimes you get asked to donate something for the silent auction at the disaster relief dinner, or sometimes you even get asked to give things away to the employees of a charitable organization. It feels good to help these organizations, and we all want to help out when we can. But here's a problem: some people think that donating their products or services will get them a nice tax deduction. The thought process is something like, "I can sell my services for $1,000, so I should get a tax deduction of the same amount for donating them." Or, "This product sells for $500, so I should get a tax deduction of $500 when I give it to the disaster relief auction." It doesn't work that way.

The reality is: a) you don't get any tax advantage for donating services, and b) for products, you can only deduct the cost of the inventory or raw materials used. To put some numbers on it, let's say you're an artist (remember Eve?), you're in a high tax bracket of 33%, and you donated a painting to a fundraiser for an environmental cause. You might value this painting at $10,000, but the materials used to make it amount to some canvas, some brushes, and some paint, which only adds up to $100. We apply your tax rate, and we see that your actual tax savings is $33, assuming you even itemized. Ouch. Sure, after the tax deduction, the total cost to the artist is $67, but if the painting took 40 hours to create, we might consider that spending 40 hours and $67 for the benefit of the donation might not be worth it. We'll examine other, more successful ideas below.

A better idea is to ask to advertise with the charitable organization, if it's one you wish to support. In the previous example our artist friend could say, "Yes, I'd love to support the environmental fundraiser! Instead of donating artwork, what I'd like to do is give you $500 and hang a banner at the event advertising my business." The $500 still goes to support the charity, but instead of a charitable contribution, the cash gets taxed as an advertising expense. You might be wondering, "Can I simply give the $500 cash as a donation and deduct it?" You can, but it most likely (talk to your tax pro) goes on your personal tax return, and never gets deducted as a business expense, which means it doesn't reduce self-employment tax (about 15%), and it doesn't reduce "above the line" income, which means it won't help with certain "phase outs" that can get quite complicated. There is also a chance you won't get any advantage at all if your personal expenses don't amount to more than the standard deduction amount (which got a lot higher beginning in 2018).

> *Hot Tax Tip*
> Charitable donations don't reduce self-employment taxes for most businesses, and they're not deductible at all unless you itemize, so it's often better to advertise with the charity rather than donate.

Let's compare some scenarios, each of which feature a charitable organization receiving cash or "donated stuff" for an event. In each scenario, we can value the goodwill (i.e., brand recognition, publicity, and awareness all rolled into one) the business receives at $2,000, and let's say the cash or the "stuff" provided to the charity is valued at $1,500. Each person is in the same 28% tax bracket. Oh, one more thing: in these examples each person is able to benefit from charitable contributions. In a lot of cases (especially under the Tax Cuts and Jobs Act), many people no longer get a tax benefit for donating to charity. Ok, let's go!

Rental Randy has a business providing tables, chairs, and place settings for events such as weddings. Randy offered to set up the event with tables and chairs, valued at $1500 for the evening. Because his contribution was a service, his tax benefit is $0, and he spent 5 hours of his own time setting up before the event. His total cost for the $2,000 of goodwill generated by the event is $1,500 plus 5 hours of his time (including opportunity cost of renting his stuff for a gig that would actually pay him for his services).

Luthier Larry built a custom guitar to be auctioned at the event. He normally sells the guitars through his website, and they go for around $1,500. His cost of materials is $500, and he spends about 20 hours making each instrument. His taxable benefit is 28% x $500, or $140. His actual cash spent was $500-$140 = $360, and to calculate his total cost, we add in his potential profit of $1000 from selling the guitar online (his opportunity cost). In total, his cost was $1,360 and 20 hours to get $2,000 worth of goodwill.

Giving Gary gave product worth $1,500 to be auctioned next to Luthier Larry's guitar. His cost for the product was $1,000, but he simply buys inventory directly from a manufacturer and resells it, so he doesn't personally spend any time with each item. His taxable benefit for the deduction is 28% x $1000 = $280. His actual cash spent was $1,000-$280 = $720, plus his opportunity cost of $500, so Gary spent $1,220 to get $2,000 worth of goodwill, but it didn't require any of Gary's time.

Advertising Amy paid the same organization $1,500 in cash to sponsor the event. Her taxable benefit is 28% x $1,500 = $420. She didn't pass up any chances to earn revenue, and she didn't spend any time except for writing a check, so her opportunity cost was $0. Thus, she spent $1,080 for $2,000 worth of recognition and goodwill, and it didn't require any of her time.

Michael A. York, EA
Andrew L. Stevens, EA, MBA

> ### Don't Go There Doug!
> Doug spent about $1000 throughout the year on various "funding" websites, where you contribute directly to people in need. When he does his taxes, he adds that figure to his other charitable contributions, and deducts the whole thing. Don't go there, Doug! Only donations to designated charities are eligible for a tax deduction.

Simply put, it's almost always better to arrange to advertise with the charity of your choice rather than to simply give them cash, products, or services.

Questions for your tax professional:
1. Do I get any benefit for donating to charity?
2. What kind of documentation do I need if I choose to advertise with a charity?
3. Why is an "above-the-line" deduction better?

Saving taxes without spending a dime: using your own stuff

Tax savings potential: $$$$

Key topics in this story:
Tax
- Deduct the value of things you already own.
- Deduct the cost of your Reference Library.
- How does "ordinary and necessary" apply to your business?

It's pretty much common knowledge that if you purchase things for your business you can write them off. "It's a write off!" What does that mean, exactly? It means you get to subtract the cost of those items from your business income, with the bottom line being that you don't pay tax on that money. In a simplified example, if you are a house painter and you buy a paint brush for $10, you don't pay tax on that $10. Let's say you earned $100 for the year (reminder: overly simplified example), and you bought that $10 paint brush. You wouldn't pay tax on the whole $100 you made, you would only pay tax on $90 of it, because you "wrote off" the cost of the paint brush.

But what about stuff you already own? What if that same painter found some brushes in his garage and decided to use those? Converting things you already own into business assets is extremely common, and pretty much everyone who goes into business has to do it. If you're reading this book on a digital reader that you bought before you went into business, you could be converting that reader into a business asset at this very moment! Let's describe how it works!

> ### Hot Tax Tip
> Converting things you already own into business assets is a way to get a great tax deduction without spending a dime!

Remember the old tale of King Midas, who was granted a wish that everything he touched turned to gold? When you create a business, you get to have the same "power" in a manner of speaking. Everything you own that you "touch" in your business could be converted into a business asset, and thus it becomes a potential tax savings. Since a penny saved is a penny earned, by converting your stuff into business assets you're practically using the Midas Touch.

Think about all the things you do and all the things you have. Every time you use one of those for business, it is now a business asset. Go home to your office and start touching things. Your desk, your lamp, your rug, your chair, your computer, and on and on. All of these things you can deduct or depreciate, depending on when you bought them, and if you legitimately use them in your business. If you bought those things this year, you can deduct them. If you bought them in the past, you can depreciate them, which simply means you get to deduct a portion of them every year for a few years.

> ### Records Check
> Any time you convert something to business use write it down in your tax ledger.

Even if you received any of these things as an inheritance (sorry, gifts don't get this tax advantage) you can "place them in service" (which just means you use them in your business) and get a nice tax savings. Here's how to do it: Make a list of everything you're placing in service and be as accurate as possible. Describe what it is exactly, when you bought or received it, how much you paid for it (or how much it was worth when you inherited it), and the percentage you use it for business. That last part is tricky – it doesn't mean how much you use it per day for business or per year. If you use it one time for five minutes for business the whole year, and otherwise it just sits around doing nothing, then you use it 100% for business. If it's your computer and you use it 6 hours per day for business and 2 hours per day for chatting with grandma, then you use it 75% for business. Be accurate and fair, and if you're not sure how much something is business versus personal use, it's a good idea to keep track of how much you use it for a month or so. Write down business use and personal use and calculate your business use percentage accordingly.

> ### Records Check
> A lot of time people think the only records the IRS cares about are receipts, but for things like business use versus personal use, or business mileage, a handwritten tax journal works just fine.

Next go to eBay, craigslist, or your other favorite used goods website and try to get a "fair market value" for the item. In other words, just try to see about what it would sell for, if you got a good price. Put that on the list as well. Here's what your list might look like:

Item	Acquired	Cost	FMV	FMV Source	% Bus Use
Desk	Mar, 2016	**$500**	$1000	Craigslist	100%
Calculator	2003	$100	**$50**	eBay	100%
Chair	2014	$75	**$25**	Craigslist	100%
Computer	Dec 2017	**$1,500**	$1,500	Darkweb	50%
Book	2006	$100	**$25**	Amazon	100%

> ### Hot Tax Tip
> Take screenshots of the reference prices you find when searching for fair market values. Save those screenshots (or print them) in your tax records.

The amount we get to use to lower our taxes is the lesser of the fair market value or the cost. If your desk was the deal of the century and it's really worth a lot more than you paid for it (see the table above), unfortunately you can only use the amount you paid for it. Likewise, old office chairs don't tend to hold their value well, and you can only use the amount that you would spend for a similar used chair.

If you're thinking "I've done all of this before," then we have one more idea for you that we bet you haven't done, and that is your "reference library." Now, education you purchased before going into business is usually not deductible, but if you have books and other reference materials on your shelves or in your closets, use that same formula above and see if you can save at least the cost of this book.

> ### *Don't Go There Doug!*
> Doug visited a garage sale, and after sorting through some old mattresses, he paid $10 for an antique desk. Later he found out it could be worth thousands of dollars, if he could find the right buyer. Rather than trying to sell the desk, Doug placed it into service in his business, and took a big tax deduction. Don't go there, Doug! Doug can only take the market value of the desk or what he paid for it, whichever is *less.* In this case, even if the desk is worth thousands, he can still only deduct $10.

Now, a word of caution. If you remember how the tale of King Midas ended, it wasn't so happy. King Midas accidentally turned his daughter to gold when she attempted to give him a comforting embrace. The King learned that if you let your Midas Touch go too far, you can end up with some very unwanted outcomes. For example, it might be unwise to say, "Oh, I use this treadmill to stay in shape, and I have to be in shape for my business selling t-shirts online, so it's a business asset!" Or, "I once watched *Fast Money* on my 70-inch tv in the living room, so that's a business asset, too!" The key words for whether something should be a business asset are "ordinary" and "necessary." It needs to be both. If you are an Uber driver, a jet ski wouldn't be an ordinary nor necessary purchase. If you are a water sports videographer, then it could be! If you use something primarily for business, and it's ordinary and necessary, then you might be eligible for a tax deduction that you didn't even know about.

Questions for your tax professional:
1. How do I place an asset into service?
2. How do I define "ordinary and necessary" for my business?
3. How do I determine business use percentage?
4. What method of deprecation is appropriate for each of my assets used in my business?

Rick and Mo's escape room business

Tax savings potential: $$$$

Key topics in this story:
Tax
- S-Corp vs. Partnership tax savings.
- How to save big bucks by buying a vehicle.

Business
- Business models to make decisions before making investments.
- Peculiarities of commercial real estate.
- Comparing potential business locations.
- Commercial real estate agents.
- Permitting.
- Hiring employees.
- Outsourcing payroll.
- Selling a business – receiving cash, equity, or a combination.

Rick and Mo were golfing buddies who enjoyed traveling together. They married women who also loved to travel, so it was a natural fit for the four of them to take vacations together. While on vacation, the group participated in an "escape room" activity. They were locked in a room for 60 minutes and had to discover clues and solve puzzles in order to escape. They had a great time, and the four of them immediately put their heads together to see if they could make this concept work as a business.

> <u>Business Tip</u>
> Start your business model well before you think you have all the information. A lot of times it will reveal all the things you don't know that you need to research.

They started by modeling the financials to see how the business could make money. At this point we're often asked, "Wait, how can you model the financials for a company you don't own yet?" The answer is, you just kind of wing it and make educated guesses and refine your model as newer and better information becomes available. Let's look at the escape room business as an example. If you're unfamiliar, it works like this: An escape room business has several themed environments where groups of people spend 60 minutes exploring and solving puzzles. The "inputs" for the model were thus pretty simple: Revenue is simply the cost of a ticket multiplied by the number of people who attend, and the cost side is all of the rent, employees, and buildout expenses of the themed rooms and the rest of the facility (lobby, bathrooms, etc.). After estimating all of the cost items they could think of, they looked at how many tickets they would need to sell on a monthly basis in order to make a profit.

While brainstorming cost categories, they searched their local market to see how many competitors there were, and they looked online for possible spaces to rent. The first thing they learned when looking at properties is that commercial real estate is **nothing** like residential real estate. In residential real estate, rent is listed as a monthly expense, plus utilities. In commercial real estate, rent is listed as the cost of renting one square foot for one year. To calculate monthly rent, you have to multiply the yearly cost of one square foot by the total number of square feet you need, and then divide by 12 months.

In addition to utilities, it is common for leases to specify the "nets" the tenant is required to pay, with double net (abbreviated NN) or triple net (NNN) being the most common, depending on your local real estate market. Each "net" represents a category of expenses the landlord requires the tenant to pay, in addition to rent. These categories are property taxes, insurance, and maintenance. In a "gross" lease, the landlord pays for those things out of the rent he or she collects, but as you can imagine this often results in higher rent per square foot.

The other thing that surprised the group was that in residential real estate, sellers and landlords go to a lot of trouble to make a home look inviting and well cared-for. In commercial real estate, often whatever shape the property was in when the last tenant moved out is the same shape it will be in when shown to prospective tenants. Rick and Mo would walk into a top-dollar property and the floors would be trashed, with holes in walls and dead cockroaches lying upside down in the corners. They found it to be bizarre. Of course, the reason is that you can negotiate for "tenant improvement," or TI. TI is any changes made to the layout, design, and finishes of a space in order to accommodate the new tenant. The cost of these improvements is often in the tens of thousands of dollars, and the landlord and business owner negotiate who pays for which part of it. Landlords don't go to a lot of trouble fixing a place up (or even cleaning) because they know the new tenant is likely to tear everything out and want something completely different.

Rick and Mo compared a few different properties, and they weighed pros and cons for each. The sheer number of properties available was very daunting, so they needed to create some "filters" to narrow their search. When renting space for any business, it's important to give a lot of thought to the type of property your business needs, and the general location where it can thrive. In nearly every town there is a storefront that serves as a revolving door for new restaurants that seem doomed to fail. Right now it's a take-out joint, six months ago it was burgers, and in another six months it will be pizza, but none of them will work. Why? It could be the location of the building. Maybe it's on an awkward corner of a one-way street, or maybe traffic always seems to be going in the opposite direction of the business (e.g., the common sight of two gas stations on opposite street corners, where one of them one of them is constantly busy while the other is a ghost town). Another issue could be the appearance of the space. There is a restaurant near Andy's (one of the authors) house that advertises itself as a quaint Italian bistro, but he's never visited because from the outside it looks like a big carpet warehouse. The point is the property a business occupies can have a big impact on how well it performs.

Michael A. York, EA
Andrew L. Stevens, EA, MBA

The escape room concept is a trendy activity, so Rick and Mo filtered their search results based on where hip and trendy people were likely to go for a night out; in other words, they were looking for a cool part of town, located near newer restaurants and bars. There are also a lot of families who play escape rooms together, so they filtered further based on locations that were family-friendly, so that meant plenty of parking, at least one family restaurant nearby, and definitely no "sketchy" areas. Their research suggested that walk-ins weren't a big part of the revenue stream, and most people purchased tickets online in advance, so street-front property with a lot of signage wasn't critical.

With their search sufficiently narrowed, Rick and Mo retained the services of a tenant-rep commercial real estate agent. They realized they didn't have the experience in commercial real estate to be certain they were negotiating every point of the lease effectively and getting the best deal possible. Tenants don't have to pay the commissions for tenant-rep real estate agents, so there was really nothing to lose. They used their common sense to screen the advice provided by their agent, and ultimately they got a great deal on a space.

> <u>Business Tip</u>
> A good tenant rep agent is always worth every penny you pay them (because you don't have to pay them!)

Next came the biggest headache many small business owners will face: Permitting. The space Rick and Mo had chosen was formerly an antiques shop, so they had to file plans and apply for permits with the city to change the occupancy designation. Nothing will make you want to bang your head against the wall quite like dealing with your city on permitting issues. Just like taxes, any laws that apply to big businesses also apply to small ones. The difference is, with taxes you simply assert that you have done things correctly, file a return, and the government has to perform an audit to show that you are wrong. With permits you have to prove that you have done things correctly, and then prove it again, and again, and then the person you were dealing with changed jobs so you have to start all over, and then when you're a week away from getting your permit a supervisor gets involved and changes something, and then someone says, "Wait, this wastewater survey is 8 months old," and you say "It was brand new when I started this whole thing!" Big businesses have armies of lawyers and contractors who specialize in permits, and as a small business owner you may have to hire specialists who can help you at city hall.

Rick and Mo networked with their tenant rep real estate agent to find people to hire for permitting, and they interviewed architects, engineers, and contractors. They conducted these interviews with the same diligence as if they were hiring a nanny for their children. They negotiated rates, they asked for references, and they asked around their network for recommendations. They knew that, ultimately, the success and speediness of this person could make or break their business. If you think that is perhaps a bit extreme, take a minute to read "Permitting nightmares: Chris' Song."

Finally, before they could open to the public, Rick and Mo needed to hire employees. They considered a few things before posting the jobs: How much they could afford to pay each employee, the skills required to do the job, the typical schedule each employee would work, and the type of personality required to interact with the general public. *(Note: When it comes to dealing with employees, we strongly recommend reading "Beth and the one function you should always outsource." Human resources issues are fraught with pitfalls, and having a trusted partner handle the legal matters can really save your bacon.)*

The particulars of employee schedules, personalities, experience, training required, etc. will be different for every business, so we won't go into too much detail about the particular choices Rick and Mo made. However, there were some very smart things they did that we would like to share. When they posted the job listings on popular online job boards, they set up a new email inbox to collect applications. It's not uncommon for a business to receive hundreds and hundreds of applications, which will clog up anyone's inbox and make it more likely for important business emails to go unnoticed. Next, after screening resumes, they conducted phone screenings with applicants to further narrow the field. They found that a great number of promising applicants were actually not a good fit for the job for reasons like living several hours away, not having a schedule that fit the needs of the business, and in more than one case, telling Rick and Mo something bizarre like, "I don't like having a boss," or, "I got fired from my last job because I'm addicted to playing games on my phone, but I'm planning to cut down starting January 1." Screening these people on the phone saved Rick and Mo from having to interview them in person.

After hiring employees and setting the schedule for a couple of weeks using sticky notes, text messages, emails, voicemails, and Facebook messages to collect time-off requests, Rick subscribed to an online service that allowed employees to input schedule requests and clock in and out using their phones. The service aggregated scheduling requests and showed who was available to work any given shift, and it sent alerts if people were late or failed to clock out on time. The service also showed the physical location of employees when they clocked in and out, and more than once Rick saw that an employee or two had clocked in while still on the freeway, or had clocked out at their home, long after their shift ended. This made it easy to adjust time cards and reprimand employees when necessary. The service also interfaced seamlessly with an online payroll service that calculated and filed payroll taxes, and orchestrated direct deposited paychecks every two weeks. It was a major time saver.

> *Business Tip*
> Payroll and other human resources tasks can quickly consume all of your time. Outsourcing them can save you time, and possibly make you money.

Ok, let's change gears and talk about some tax topics. Rick and Mo originally structured their business as a partnership, and thus they paid income tax and self-employment tax on all of the proceeds after expenses. However, by changing their structure to an S-Corporation, they were able to legally avoid some taxes. Here's how: Partnership profits (for general partners) are subject to income tax and self-employment tax, and they "flow through" the partnership and end up getting taxed on each partner's individual tax return. In other words, the partnership itself files a tax return, but it doesn't actually pay any taxes. Instead the taxes get paid by the individual partners. On the flip side, as a shareholder in an S-Corporation, the proceeds are only subject to income tax. Profits still flow through to the shareholder's individual tax return, but unlike partnership profits, they're not subject to self-employment tax, which is about 15%. How is that possible? It's because of some subtle differences between the legalities of corporations vs partnerships (which are beyond the scope of this book). But in short, when you own an S-Corp you are simultaneously working for the company and a shareholder, so you have to

The "Not a Tax Book" Tax Book

divide your earnings between what is a reasonable payment for the work you performed and what is fair as a return on your investment, and this will be different for every company. However, the key thing to know is that the proceeds that are paid out as return on investment are not subject to self-employment tax. That is potentially a big savings.

> *Hot Tax Tip*
> Choosing the right type of entity for your business can save big bucks.

In Rick and Mo's case, the work they performed was very basic and simple, like answering phones and occasionally conducting a job interview. Since this was a side-business, they weren't actively at the location every day – they had employees who handled most of that. They calculated what they would pay someone else to do the jobs they performed, and compensated themselves based on that figure, which was subject to self-employment tax in the form of FICA. The remainder of their profits were investment returns, and thus not subject to self-employment tax.

> *Don't Go There Doug!*
> Doug owns his own S-Corp professional firm, and he wants to pay as little self-employment tax as possible. He signs a contract with his firm where he agrees to work for minimum wage, even though he bills his clients $500 per hour. Don't go there, Doug! S-Corp owner compensation has to be reasonable, and Doug would have a tough time convincing anyone that it's reasonable to pay a minimum wage salary to a professional who bills $500 per hour.

Obviously, this is a strategy that some people have taken advantage of, like a lawyer who paid himself very little for working 60 hours per week as an attorney. As you can imagine if you're working 60 hours per week as a lawyer, you can't say that the money you earned was due to something other than the time and effort you put in (after all, lawyers make money by billing for their time), and thus all of your profit would be subject to self-employment tax. The IRS is hip to the ways people try to abuse this strategy, so the important thing is to pay a reasonable wage for the time and effort spent running the business. This is one such way that a change in entity type can have a big tax savings, so talk to your tax professional to see if this is something that might work for you.

At the end of their first year Rick and Mo were thinking about how much more work would need to be done to build out the other escape rooms in their facility. They concluded that they needed a vehicle that could haul tools, lumber, furniture, and other props and materials to and from their location. They looked at new and used trucks and SUVs and settled on a new SUV. Because the new SUV was over 6,000 lbs. of "Gross Vehicle Weight" (GVW), it qualified for special tax treatment – basically, any new or used SUV over 6,000 lbs. GVW qualifies for 100% "bonus depreciation," meaning you get to deduct the entire cost of the vehicle in the first year, up to the percentage the vehicle is used for business. In other words, if you use it 90% for business, you get to deduct 90% of the cost in the first year.

Rick and Mo bought the vehicle for $50,000 in December, and they kept logs of the miles they drove. From the day they bought the vehicle until December 31 they used it 100% for business (they each had other vehicles they used for personal errands), and thus they were able to deduct 100% of the $50,000 cost, which lowered their tax liability considerably.

> *Hot Tax Tip*
> Purchasing a business vehicle can add up to big tax savings, but
> this is an area you shouldn't explore without the help of a qualified
> tax professional!

After three years of growth, Rick and Mo decided to sell their business. They had started families, and the business deserved more attention than they had available. It was time to find a buyer. The first thing they did was value the business using rigorous methods like Discounted Free Cash Flow analysis, and using common valuation multiples on revenue and EBITDA (earnings before interest, taxes, depreciation, and amortization). All of that is beyond the scope of this book, and ultimately it doesn't matter all that much because anything is worth only as much as someone else is willing to pay for it. Rick and Mo put out feelers online for escape room owners, and they networked with people they had met in the industry. After some conversations they received two offers, both lower than they were hoping for (per usual).

There are generally two types of business sales – cash and equity. In a cash sale the buyer gives the seller cash in exchange for the business. In an equity sale the buyer gives the seller shares (ownership) in the new business. Equity deals typically shift risk from the buyer to the seller, because the seller shares in the success or failure of the deal, but that risk shifting also typically results in a higher price paid by the buyer. In many cases, deals are a combination of cash and equity. At least, they are in corporate America where big companies are listed on public stock exchanges. When Rick and Mo received the low offers, they had a decision to make – take the low offers (after negotiating for more, of course), keep the business and hope to get a higher offer later, or negotiate some kind of equity deal. Now, in small deals like this one an equity deal is pretty uncommon for a number of reasons, but that doesn't mean it's impossible. Rick and Mo presented the buyers with some options, and ultimately they settled on a deal where they would get a smaller upfront cash payment, but they would also receive a royalty based on sales for a period of time after the sale. This meant if the business did well Rick and Mo would get more than the original cash offer, and it reduced the risk for the buyer because if the business didn't perform as expected they wouldn't have spent as much to acquire it.

> ### Business Tip
> Agreeing to finance the sale of your business often means you can get a higher price for the business, but it also means you take on additional risk with the sale. However, because cash paid upfront is less, the deal is more affordable for more buyers, which means you might find yourself in a bidding war.

Let's recap. Rick and Mo stumbled upon what was then a novel idea for a business, and they learned a great deal about renting real estate, hiring employees, and permitting. They strategized with their attorney and their tax professional to change the type of their business entity to an S-Corporation, which lowered the amount of tax they paid, and they chose a business vehicle based on what would give them the biggest and most immediate tax benefit. In the end they sold their business, and rather than take a small cash payment up front, they negotiated to take a slightly smaller cash payment with a royalty trail that could add up to a great deal more money over time.

Questions for your tax professional:
1. What if I use my business vehicle less than 50% for business?
2. What constitutes business use of a vehicle, and how can I document my business miles?
3. Would it benefit me to be an S-corporation in my business?
4. What is reasonable compensation for my business?
5. Do you have a payroll company you recommend?
6. What are the tax implications of selling my business?

Permitting nightmares: Chris's Song
Tax savings potential: $

Key topics in this story:
Business
- Temper your expectations when it comes to city hall.
- Hire professionals to handle permitting issues whenever possible.
- Find a "grandfathered" permit whenever possible.

Chris moved into a new house, and immediately his new neighbors told him to keep his garage locked at night and to install a security camera on his front porch. He was astounded – his house was on a quiet street in a safe part of town, so why the need for all of the vigilance? His neighbors told him about the liquor store three streets over, and how undesirables tended to radiate out from it, leaving trash in their wake, urinating in yards, and occasionally stealing tools or breaking into a car. Chris resigned himself to the fact that the liquor store would be there forever, and he put up the cameras.

To his great joy, a few months later Chris noticed that "for lease" signs were in the liquor store windows. This was great news, and Chris discussed it with his neighbors. They wanted something family friendly that would fit with their idea of the neighborhood, and an ice cream shop seemed like the perfect thing. They decided that the best thing to do would be to put together a pitch and take it to a local ice cream business, and hope the owner would consider opening a second location. They also put together some funds to offer as an incentive, either as a loan or an investment, to sweeten the deal. The owner of the ice cream shop loved the idea, and they set wheels in motion to kick the liquor store out of the neighborhood.

To cut to the chase, they signed a lease with the landlord contingent on permitting, and they planned to spend about $40k on improvements to bring the space up to code, and another $25k to update the "curb appeal" of the building. They hired an architect who made drawings to show City Hall their plans for the space. Because the occupancy was changing from a liquor store to an ice cream store, city code required investment in upgrading the property for the new use. Improvements such as a new fire sprinkler system and HVAC upgrades were going to be expensive. The final hurdle was parking. Per city code, twelve spots were required for the new occupancy class, but the existing parking lot had eight spaces.

The city's calculations predicted that a restaurant of the size of the ice cream shop would receive an average of 12 guests per hour, requiring 12 parking spots. The owner disagreed. First, he appealed to logic: Unlike a restaurant, people don't spend much time at an ice cream shop. An average person might spend an hour at a small deli, but about 30 minutes at an ice cream parlor. By that logic, each of those twelve people would be in the shop for a maximum of 30 minutes, necessitating only six parking spots. The math was sound, but the city didn't budge. The city planner insisted that the "parking overflow" would annoy neighbors. "Would it be more annoying than the constant stream of vagrants coming and going from the liquor store?" The city didn't share an opinion on that.

Michael A. York, EA
Andrew L. Stevens, EA, MBA

The next option was to get a code variance, and they would need to attend the next variance approval meeting in order to do so. Meetings in this municipality were held quarterly, you had to apply two quarters in advance, and after that it could take another quarter to get a decision, and even then it would be a few more months before permits would be issued. Getting a variance could take over a year in this bureaucratic nightmare, with no guarantee of success. Chris went to all of his neighbors and got over a hundred signatures asking to bypass the process, but the city wasn't convinced. Chris and friends tried arguing that crime would be reduced in the area, thus driving up property values and increasing the tax base, while also reducing the need for police presence in the area, but still the city insisted on four more parking spots.

Eventually the ice cream store owner ran out of money and patience and abandoned the idea of a new store at that location. Of course, there was one class of occupant that was "grandfathered" in to the existing permit, a liquor store, and a new one opened in the neighborhood within a few months.

To recap, by replacing the liquor store with an ice cream shop the neighborhood would have been improved, property values would have increased, crime would have decreased, and an old building would have been brought up to present-day safety standards. There was no downside, except getting rid of a cheap liquor store that was on the outskirts of town when it was built 50 years prior. And yet, because of permitting issues it's still a liquor store, and people nearby still lock their garages at night and catch strangers urinating on their flower beds on a fairly regular basis.

Is there a moral to this story, or at least one piece of helpful advice we can take away? We suppose that the best thing to learn is to have as much patience as possible when dealing with permitting issues, find a "grandfathered" occupancy whenever possible, hire professionals, and budget more time and money to get permits than you think you need. Permitting is one of those issues that new business owners tend to overlook, and experienced business owners shudder when thinking about. We think that everyone should expect the worst when dealing with their city's permitting office, and that way they will be pleasantly surprised if things go smoothly.

> ### *Don't Go There Doug!*
> Doug is about to sign a lease for a new business location, and he's concerned about permitting. His landlord told him not to worry, plenty of his other tenants have opened their businesses while still going through the permitting process. Don't go there, Doug! Don't trust the landlord's word on this one. If you have to sign a lease, at the very least get it in writing that the lease is null and void if permits cannot be obtained.

What does this story have to do with taxes? (If you think there isn't a way to make everything about taxes then you definitely don't think like a tax savant yet). Chris's local liquor store eviction didn't work out, but the ice cream store was able to deduct the expenses incurred in attempting to expand their business, even though ultimately they didn't open the second location. Additionally, depending on how Chris structured his activities in opening the ice cream store, he could have claimed some deductions and saved some tax, though he would have needed to get his tax professional involved early on in order to make sure he conducted himself correctly.

Questions for your tax professional:
1. What are start-up costs and organizational costs?
2. My business failed before it made any money, can I deduct anything?
3. What expenses can I deduct as an investor or limited partner?

Michael A. York, EA
Andrew L. Stevens, EA, MBA

Yolanda lets her business pay for her family's medical expenses

Tax savings potential: $$$

Key topics in this story:
Tax
- Medical reimbursement plans.
- How to get a tax deduction for out-of-pocket medical expenses.

Of all the strategies in this book, this is the one that earns us the most pushback from our clients. It sounds like a loophole that the IRS will close any second now. In fact, this strategy has been around for years, and at least three Presidents (each signing their own tweaks to the tax code) have left it intact. We're confident this loophole will be around for a while to come.

Let's meet Yolanda. Yolanda has a regular job where she has great benefits, including health care. She has a side business where she tutors kids in math and science, as well as teaching music lessons. Yolanda is married, and she and her wife (Isabella) have a daughter with diabetes. A lot of their daughter's medical care is covered by health insurance, but there are still loads and loads of out of pocket costs that Yolanda and Isabella have to cover every month. Between deductibles, copayments, mileage to and from doctor's offices, and over-the-counter medications, out-of-pocket medical expenses add up fast. In fact, the reason Yolanda started her tutoring business in the first place was to cover these costs. Yolanda was thrilled when we told her that not only could her earnings from the business pay these costs, but the business could pay them directly and get a tax deduction.

Yolanda was excited, then skeptical. Here's why: What we proposed to Yolanda was something called a Medical Reimbursement Plan. A Medical Reimbursement Plan (MRP) allows a business owner to reimburse employees' out-of-pocket medical expenses, without taxing the employee, and while providing a deduction for the business.

Yolanda said, "Ok, but I don't have employees."

We said, "Yes, but the plan doesn't have to cover just employees, it also covers their families."

"Not only do I not have employees, I don't have an employee with a family," Yolanda replied.

"What if you hired your wife?" we asked. "Then the plan would cover your wife and her family, which includes you and your daughter."

"That sounds aggressive – I don't want to get audited," Yolanda said.

"These plans have been around so long that there are well-respected, national companies that provide the paperwork and all the administration for a very small fee."

"It sounds like a loophole that will get closed as soon as I sign up," she said.

"These plans have been popular for well over a decade, and they don't seem to be going anywhere any time soon."

Yolanda contacted an MRP provider, and she has been using it ever since. Let's look at how she uses it.

First, Yolanda hired her wife, Isabella. Yolanda decided she needed help with her website, answering the phone, basic marketing, and light clean-up of her home office where she met with clients. She and Isabella agreed that minimum wage was fair for those duties, considering the extra financial benefit Isabella would receive in the form of reimbursed medical expenses for herself and her family (which, again, includes Yolanda and their daughter).

Don't Go There Doug!
Doug "hired" his spouse in his business, but he never deposits money into her bank account, doesn't issue a W-2, and doesn't have an employment contract. Don't go there, Doug! If you are going to hire your spouse, have a solid employment contract, and make sure you pay and report wages like you would for any other employee!

Then, at the end of every month, Isabella totals up the family's out-of-pocket medical costs and submits receipts to her medical reimbursement plan administrator. The administrator then instructs Yolanda to reimburse the expenses, which she does by cutting a check to Isabella. The expenses don't have to be the same for every month: one month Isabella reimbursed herself for Yolanda's reading glasses, and the next month she submitted receipts for some nose strips her doctor recommended she wear while she sleeps. The plan administrator provided a large list of all of the deductible expenses, which comes in very handy.

Now, you might be saying, "Wait, didn't Yolanda simply take her business's money and pay her personal expenses?" Yes, she did, but by structuring things correctly, and by jumping through a few hoops, she gets a tax deduction for it. This is the reality of the United States tax code.

Let's look at the tax deduction Yolanda receives from this strategy. She pays Isabella for the work she performs, but that's a wash because they're married (all of the money is "their" money anyway). She isn't required to withhold federal or state income tax from Isabella's paycheck, but she is required to pay Social Security and Medicare tax on Isabella's hourly wages (not including reimbursed medical expenses). On the other hand, Yolanda gets to deduct all of the family's out-of-pocket medical expenses that otherwise wouldn't be deductible due to her income level. Not only are those expenses deductible with this plan, but they're deductible against federal income tax, state income tax, and self-employment tax! In Yolanda's case she saves forty percent, and plenty of people save a lot more than that!

Yolanda's plan administrator helps her with the paperwork, and they charge a reasonable (and deductible) fee, which is less than $500 per year. They even guarantee that the plan is audit-proof!

MRPs are best for small businesses, and there are a lot of complications that can arise when the business is structured as a partnership or corporation, or if the business has more employees than just the owner's spouse. With that in mind, we recommend that our readers talk to their tax professional if they think this might benefit them. We also recommend that our clients think very carefully about whether their spouse can be a legitimate employee in their business, because if the answer is "no," then this plan simply isn't for them. However, as we say all the time, if you have a small business you have to have all of the same functions as any big business, like marketing, accounting, human resources, and so on. The difference is, all of those responsibilities fall on you to execute. In Yolanda's case she was glad to pass off some of those responsibilities to her wife, who is a natural when it comes to web development, marketing, and content creation. It was easy to make the case that Isabella is a legitimate employee.

Questions for your tax professional:
1. Could I benefit from setting up a medical reimbursement account and hiring my spouse?
2. How much out-of-pocket medical expenses do I need before I can benefit from a tax deduction on my schedule A?
3. How much would I save if I could deduct my out of pocket medical expenses against my business income?

Michael A. York, EA
Andrew L. Stevens, EA, MBA

How Dinesh and Maxine got creative with employee business expenses

Tax savings potential: $$$

Key topics in this story:
Tax
- How to deduct non-deductible employee business expenses
- How to replace a taxable bonus with non-taxable reimbursements
- How to deduct the expenses of S-Corp owners

Dinesh has been a client for ages, and we recently met his employer, Maxine. Dinesh is a graphic designer, and he is an employee at Maxine's architecture firm that does amazing renovations of old hotels. Maxine's firm pays for most of Dinesh's expenses with respect to his employment, but there are some books and other materials he purchases every year that help him stay up to date on the latest graphic design software and he usually takes a trip in the summer to a big conference where he networks with other graphic design professionals and learns from them. Maxine's firm doesn't pay for these expenses, but until recently Dinesh could deduct them on his tax return and get a nice tax savings.

When the Tax Cuts and Jobs Act was signed into law it removed the tax benefit of employee business expenses, which caused a lot of people to make decisions about what employment expenses they were going to continue to pay for. The next year Dinesh was looking at the expensive books he usually buys, and the conference he travels to, and he was re-evaluating whether he could afford those expenses without getting a tax break for them.
Dinesh told us about his predicament, and we reviewed the breakdown of his compensation for the year. In addition to his salary, Dinesh also receives a yearly performance bonus, and this gave us an idea. We suggested to Dinesh that he could ask his employer if she could pay for his books and conference expenses instead of paying his yearly bonus, which worked out to about the same amount of money.

"Isn't that the same thing?" He asked.

"No!" We said.

64

Here's how it's not the same thing: If Dinesh gets a bonus, he pays federal income tax, plus state income tax, plus FICA tax on the full amount of the bonus. His employer is also responsible for payroll taxes on the bonus that Dinesh receives. However, if instead Maxine were to reimburse Dinesh for his books and conference expenses, then Dinesh would not get taxed on the reimbursement, and Maxine would save on payroll taxes. It's a win-win. Let's look at an example:

In a typical year, Dinesh's bonus works out like this:

Bonus amount:	$5,000
Fed Income tax:	$1,000
State Income tax:	$ 250
Payroll tax:	$ 383
Total bonus after tax:	**$3,367**
Maxine's cost:	**$5,383**

On the other hand, if Maxine reimburses Dinesh for his expenses, the math breaks down like this (assuming everything costs $5,000 just to keep this an apples-to-apples comparison).

Reimbursed expenses:	$5,000
Fed, State, FICA taxes:	$ 0
Total "Bonus":	**$5,000**
Maxine's cost:	**$5,000**

See? Everyone is better off! Why doesn't everyone do this, you might be wondering? Well, it involves almost five minutes of paperwork on the part of the employer, and until recently employees could simply deduct their job expenses on their tax return.

What we're talking about is called an accountable plan. An accountable plan is a way for companies to reimburse employee business expenses without including the reimbursement on the employee's W2. In other words, the employee doesn't pay tax on the reimbursement, and neither does the company.

Now, Dinesh's expenses don't exactly equal the amount of his bonus, but that's a matter for him to negotiate with Maxine. He could negotiate a smaller bonus alongside his newly-reimbursed book and conference expense, for example.

If you're an employer reading this, you might be a little agnostic about this idea. Sure, it saves a little payroll tax, but it also means you have to do some paperwork and maintain a few records. However, the upside is that you can take advantage of it, too! In fact, the S-Corp, one of the most popular entities for small businesses, says that owners don't get to deduct their own "employee" expenses against their salaries unless they have an Accountable Plan. If you would like to take advantage of a home office deduction, education and training, etc., an Accountable Plan might not just benefit your employees – you could end up personally saving a bunch of money, too!

> ### Don't Go There Doug!
> Doug thinks that as long as his accountable plan says he can be reimbursed for something, then it's fair game. So he puts his gaming system, his dog food, and his son's minibike in the accountable plan and deducts them as business expenses. Don't go there, Doug! Accountable plans can only be used for ordinary and necessary business expenses, not for any old personal expense your employer agrees to reimburse.

NOTE: You might have read this story and thought, "My business is not an S-Corp, it's an LLC. Well, an LLC doesn't exist for federal tax purposes. Instead, LLCs get taxed as partnerships, S-Corps, or as sole proprietorships. If you're not sure, ask your tax professional.

> **Questions for your tax professional:**
> 1. Can I use an Accountable Plan in my business?
> 2. What expenses are deductible in an accountable plan?
> 3. Would I benefit if my employer establishes an accountable plan?

A tale of two landlords: Short-Term Sam and Long-Term Linda

Many people know the value of investing in real estate, but being a landlord is not an easy job. Not only are properties expensive, they can quickly turn into money pits. Understanding the tax implications of real estate (and how you can strategize to keep more of the money your investments generate) will help you run your real estate business as efficiently as possible.

Before we get into it, let's discuss two common types of residential real estate investment: Long-term residential rentals, and short-term residential rentals. A long-term rental is typically a house, townhouse, or condominium that is leased on a contract lasting six months or more. Short term rentals have always been around, but they have exploded in popularity as alternatives to hotels, and they utilize online inventory and reservation platforms (and mobile apps) to connect landlords with tenants. Airbnb and VRBO are two common platforms for short term rentals.

These two types of real estate "businesses" work very differently in terms of tax and business strategies, even though both can be stand-alone units or parts of people's homes they have converted to rentals, like a basement apartment. We have profiled two different people to show you how each type works. Of course, there are opportunities to invest in commercial properties, but except for Qualified Opportunity Zones (QOZs) that is beyond the scope of this book.

Michael A. York, EA
Andrew L. Stevens, EA, MBA

Long-Term Linda

Tax savings potential: $$$$

Key topics in this story:
Tax
- Bank accounts and records for rental properties.
- Mileage deduction for landlords.
- Scouting trips to find new rental property.
- Travel to check on rental properties.
- Available to rent vs rented.
- How to stay in your own vacation rental without making it personal.
- Hiring your kids to work on your rental property.
- Placing assets into service in a rental property.

Business
- Leverage: When a business borrows money.

After being a homeowner for a few years, Linda decided it was time to upgrade from her starter home. To her great pleasure, she found that her city's current real estate cycle was in a "buyer's market," where prices were down, inventory was high, and buyers had a lot of power in negotiating the price of a house. This meant Linda had a lot of great houses to choose from, and she was able to negotiate a great deal for her new place. To her dismay, in this buyer's market, selling her old house became a real problem. It sat on the market for weeks, and her only offers were low-ball attempts at getting the house for far below the asking price. Linda covered both mortgages for a month or two, and finally asked her real estate agent about turning the house into a rental. The agent helped list the house as a rental, and within a few weeks a new family had moved in.

All the issues that come along with renters are somewhat beyond the scope of this book, but let's just summarize with this advice: Get references, check them, and then check to make sure they're real references. Then pull credit reports. Never go with your gut feeling, always go with the facts (unless your gut says "Heck, no." Then, go with the gut!). Everyone knows that the real estate market goes up and down like the stock market, but we like to coach our first-time real estate investors that renters themselves are sort of like the stock market as well. When you have a great renter it's like the stock market going up and up and up: It's easy to fall into the "trap" where you think this is how it's always going to be. However, just as the stock market is bound to enter a bear market eventually, renters are bound to move out, and it's possible that your next renter will be a "bear" renter, not to mention the possibility of the roof leaking or the foundation needing repair. The point is, successful real estate investors have the patience and the cash to weather these storms, and we recommend that our landlord clients maintain a significant cash reserve for each rental property, and don't add to their real estate portfolio until they can fully support that property's cash needs.

The first thing Linda did when she started renting her house was establish a new bank account for her new rental real estate business. She knew it is incredibly easy to co-mingle house-related expenses, and not only is that bad from a record keeping perspective, it's also a great way to miss out on a lot of deductions. Even a few days later it's difficult to remember which things you bought at the home improvement store were for your personal house versus your rental property. Having a separate bank account makes it easy to keep things tidy and not forget any deductions.

> *Hot Tax Tip*
> If you already have a bank account with a given bank, it usually only takes five minutes online to set up a new bank account for your small business.

Next, Linda downloaded a business mileage app to keep track of the miles she drove that were related to her rental property. Many landlords forget about their mileage deduction, but Linda knew that her trips to the home improvement store, her trips to check on the property, to pick up rent, or to the bank to make a deposit are all deductions that can add up to real savings.

The income Linda earned from her rental property was enough to pay her mortgage and cover any upkeep requirements, and after a few years the market in her area flipped to a seller's market, and suddenly her property was valued at a lot more than it had been a few years before. Linda took out an equity loan against the property and used the funds to purchase a new rental condominium a short flight away, right on the beach (See: "A note on leverage" below). Linda managed this new property just like her other one, with a separate bank account, sufficient reserve funds, and separate expense tracking and record keeping. However, because this other house was in a totally different city, Linda was able to take advantage of some additional tax strategies.

First, Linda traveled to three different cities to scout locations for her new rental property. Once she purchased a place, her trip to that city to scout locations became deductible. She couldn't deduct the other two scouting trips, but she understood why – the IRS is hip to the game of disguising "personal" travel as rental property scouting trips.

Next, the tax code allows for a deductible trip to visit a rental property one time per year, so Linda was able to visit the beach town where her rental property was located and deduct her airfare and other travel expenses in the process. Of course, there are circumstances where Linda might have to travel to the property more frequently, but as long as the reason for the trips was ordinary and necessary and had profit motive, then the additional trips could be deductible as well.

Like a lot of beach communities, the summer months were extremely busy, and the winter was dead as can be, with nothing but gusting winds and rainstorms instead of sea breeze and sunshine. Even though she typically rented the condo for six months at a time, the place was technically available for rent all year. Many people believe that the expenses for their rental property are only deductible if the place is rented, but expenses are deductible as long as the property is available to rent.

> *Hot Tax Tip*
> Expenses for a rental property are deductible as long as the property is available to rent, even if it is currently vacant.

The tax code allows Linda to stay in her condo up to 14 days per year without it becoming a "personal" property, so Linda typically visited her condo twice per year: once just before the busy summer season (before her tenants moved in), and once just after her tenants moved out in the fall. On each of these trips Linda tended to stay in the condo for about 10 days. Wait, what? Isn't that 20 days? Well, days spent doing maintenance don't count toward the 14-day rule, so typically in the fall Linda would spend about three days cleaning and fixing things, and then seven days relaxing on the beach. Likewise, in the spring, Linda spent seven days on the beach and her final three days fixing the place up for her new tenant.

Don't Go There Doug!
Doug lets his family members stay at his beach rental whenever they want, and they stay for free, even though they have broken the dishwasher three times. Not only do his relatives stay in the beach house, Doug uses all of his allowed days as well. Don't go there, Doug! Renting to family members has its own rules, and unless you structure things correctly (including charging and collecting every penny of fair market rent) your family members' stays will count as your own personal use, and you might lose out on a lot of rental deductions!

Hot Tax Tip
Be very careful if you let relatives stay in your rental property. Unless you do things correctly their stay counts as your stay, even if they pay you. Talk to your tax professional before you let family stay at your place!

On at least one of these trips every year Linda brought along her daughter, who helped with the cleaning, painting, and minor repairs. Linda paid her daughter a reasonable wage, and because her daughter was under seventeen, she didn't have to pay FICA tax on the earnings. The standard deduction wiped out any income tax, and thus this money was tax free to the daughter, even though Linda was able to claim a deduction for the wages. Linda next decided that the best use of the money her daughter earned was to save for retirement and college, so they deposited half the money in a Roth IRA, and the other half in a 529 college savings account. Linda's daughter never had to pay tax on this money, and if she uses the cash for retirement or college, respectively, she won't have to pay any tax on any withdrawals that she makes from those accounts (assuming tax laws don't change, of course).

> ### Hot Tax Tip
> Hiring your kids to work on your rental property can provide them with tax-free income you can use to finance their retirement or college. The "reasonable" wage you pay them should be comparable to what you would pay a stranger for similar work, but be sure to talk to your tax professional to make sure you're in the right range.

When Linda scouted the local rental market, she noticed that most of the units were furnished, and that furnished units tended to rent for higher rates and rent out more quickly. She had two choices – purchase furniture and goods for the property or place her own "stuff" into service. She did a combination of the two things. First, she went through her kitchen and packaged up all of her old dishes and pots and pans. For small items like these she was able to take a complete deduction of the fair market value in the year she "placed them into service" in her rental property. For bigger items like furniture, she was able to depreciate the fair market value (or purchase price, whichever is less). Then Linda went out and purchased new stuff for her main house, and she felt like the tax break for converting her old stuff into business assets gave her a discount on the new stuff. In fact, she figured she could do the same thing over again once the old stuff in the rental unit had completely depreciated.

> *Hot Tax Tip*
> You can buy new furniture for your rental property, or you can buy yourself new furniture for your main home, and move your old furniture into the rental property and depreciate the fair market value or cost, whichever is lower.

To recap, Linda converted her house into a rental property and made a little bit of money as a landlord. In the meantime, the property appreciated in value, and Linda took out an equity loan to purchase a condo on the beach, which is available to rent all year, but is only rented about six months or so. Linda is able to deduct her expenses for both properties, including her travel expenses for one trip per year to her beach condo. She's also able to stay in her condo for two weeks per year, plus maintenance days, and she can take a deduction for paying her daughter to clean, which her daughter can use to save for retirement or college, tax free.

One important caveat to long-term rentals: Being the owner of a long-term rental is considered a "passive activity," meaning it's not something you actively manage on a day to day basis. You might disagree, but you're going to have a tough time if want to battle the IRS on this particular issue. Because it's a passive activity, if you make over $100,000 in income, your "losses" from your rental activity are limited, and if you make over $150,000 you can only break even, even if you "lost" money on your rental property throughout the year. Now, you get to save up these disallowed losses and use them in a future year (called carryforwards). The important thing to know is that if you're a person with a high income, owning rental properties might be a great investment, but it isn't a good way to reduce your taxes (by taking losses against your other income) unless you happen to work as a real estate professional.

A note on leverage: The concept of "leverage" in a business is a confusing and scary one. Imagine borrowing most of the money to start your business, with the promise of paying it back over time, and the threat of bankruptcy looming over your head constantly. The upside to leverage is that you can start a much bigger business than you could otherwise (because you have more money to invest in the business), and you can do so without giving away equity (ownership) to investors. Taking out a mortgage to buy an investment property is exactly the same as taking out a business loan to fund your business, it's just that most people are way more comfortable with the idea of a mortgage than they are with the idea of a business loan.

> **Questions for your tax professional:**
> 1. What is the difference between personal property and an investment property?
> 2. How can my family members use my vacation rental without it being treated as my own personal stay?
> 3. What steps should I take to make sure that paying my children is deductible?
> 4. How do I know the difference between a maintenance day and a personal day?
> 5. How do passive activity loss limits impact me?
> 6. How do I determine what is an "ordinary and necessary" expense for a rental property?
> 7. What is a real estate professional for purposes of taking losses on a rental property?

Short-Term Sam

Tax savings potential: $$$$$

Key topics in this story:
Tax
- Active management of short-term rentals.
- Available to rent vs rented.
- Renting out a private residence for less than 14 days.
- Self-employment tax on active short-term rental profits.
- Section 179 deduction for active short-term rentals.
- Placing assets into service.
- Business travel for short-term rentals.

Business
- Managing a rental – tenant issues.

Short term Sam owns some rental properties just like Linda, but he manages them in a totally different way. Instead of finding tenants who will live in the properties for months at a time, he uses Airbnb to find tenants who only want to stay in his properties for a few days at a time, kind of like a hotel. Sam's case and Linda's case are very similar, except for a few key differences.

Remember at the end of Linda's story how we had to insert that caveat about how if you make over $100,000 in income, your "losses" from your rental property are limited? That doesn't apply to Sam. The short-term nature of his rentals means that he is actively managing them, and thus the passive activity loss limitations don't apply to him.

Anyway, let's get to know Sam's situation a little bit. Sam lives in a city that sees a good bit of tourist activity, convention visitors, and every February a big film festival comes to town. Sam saved up for down payments on four condos near Main Street in his city, which is a very desirable area. He furnished the condos, took pictures, and advertised them for rent online. He also lives in a townhouse near Main Street, but in a separate development from the others. His four condos are available to rent 365 days per year, and thus all of his expenses for them are deductible (if they were available for fewer days per year he might have to pro-rate his expenses). Sam raises the rent considerably during the film festival (when movie stars with deep pockets come to town), and during Bike Week, when the town is overrun by bikers who party and cause all kinds of mayhem. Sam is very careful to adjust the rates to be competitive and make sure his units rent out during the very profitable film festival, but during bike week he raises the rent in order to make sure he can afford to fix any damage his tenants cause. If the units aren't rented that's ok, at least they were available (and thus he can still deduct his expenses for those days, like mortgage interest, taxes, etc.).

During the film festival, Sam rents out his personal townhouse for 14 days and makes a killing. He can't leave town because he still has to manage his properties, but he couch-surfs for those 14 days. Because he's renting out his primary residence, and because it's rented for 14 days or fewer, Sam doesn't have to pay tax on any of the money he makes renting out his home. He doesn't even have to report it. This is often called "the Masters exemption," because people who live in mansions near a certain golf course rent out their homes for astronomical rates during the a famous golf tournament and pay zero taxes. Isn't it surprising that very influential people have been given this tax break? We're not surprised either, but we're glad that the rest of us can use this same strategy!

> ### Hot Tax Tip
> If you rent your personal home out for 14 days (or less) you never have to report that income! It's free money!

Like Linda, Sam has separate bank accounts for his rental properties, and he makes sure to put the money from renting out his personal townhouse in his personal account to make sure he doesn't report it as income by mistake. Linda could take advantage of this strategy as well, she just doesn't have the same opportunity as Sam, although she did once rent her personal house to her employer for an evening for the company Christmas party, and she didn't have to report that income, either.

The major downside of Sam's decision to rent his condos as short-term properties instead of long-term properties is that Sam has to pay the dreaded Self-Employment Tax on any profit he makes. If you're unfamiliar, think of the FICA box on your W2 that represents the Social Security and Medicare tax you pay. Now double it. That's self-employment tax.

The nature of Sam's short term, active rental business means that he can take advantage of some strategies that Linda can't. For example, Sam can deduct the cost of his home office. He can also take advantage of something called the "section 179 deduction." As much as we've tried to avoid quoting code sections, this one is a big one. Let's look at how the section 179 deduction benefits Sam compared to Linda. If Sam and Linda both decide to purchase something for their rental properties, let's say an 80" plasma screen television, they get very different tax deductions. Linda is only able to deduct a percentage of the cost of her television every year for five years. Sam, however, can choose to deduct the television over five years like Linda, or he can choose to deduct the entire cost of the television the year he bought it, using the section 179 deduction. A big tax deduction now is generally better than a series of smaller deductions taken in future years, so we're big fans of this deduction. NOTE: As we're writing this there is something called "bonus depreciation" that Sam and Linda could take advantage of, but it's a temporary thing in the tax code. As usual, talk to your tax professional.

> ### Hot Tax Tip
> Short term rentals are subject to self-employment tax, but they also can allow you to deduct a home office or even use big tax savers like the section 179 deduction.

Remember when we talked about placing assets into service using the "Midas Touch?" Well when Sam was furnishing his rental properties, he basically did the same thing. He went through his house and found furniture, televisions, gaming systems, and other things he was no longer using and that he thought would benefit his rental business, and he placed those things into service, getting a nice tax deduction for doing so.

> ### Don't Go There Doug!
> Doug bought a television, coffee maker, and a (cursed) goat statue for his rental unit, but he only installed them for a day and took some photos for his "records." Doug then moved all of the nice stuff into his house. Don't go there, Doug! The IRS is smart when it comes to those kinds of scams, and they can search for your rental listings to see what amenities you offer. If the big TV and furniture aren't in your pictures and your ads, expect the IRS to disallow the deduction.

It's critical that Sam keeps up with the overall market for short term rentals, and he occasionally visits other cities to see how other landlords market and outfit their properties. He knows (and the IRS knows, too) that traveling frequently wouldn't make sound business sense. However, Sam travels only once per year to a new city to check out a few short-term rentals, meet the owners, exchange information with them, and use that information to improve his profitability. He plans and documents his travels just like Javier, who has his own story all about business travel.

Every once in a while, usually after one of these trips, Sam feels it's necessary to overhaul some of the items in his condos. An owner in another city explained to Sam how upgrading the appliances in the units would lead to quicker rentals at a higher asking rate. Sam was surprised, but he understood the business concept: his condos compete not only against other similar short-term rental units, they also compete against hotels in the area. He would have to upgrade certain things here and there to keep pace. He couldn't afford to purchase new TVs, coffee makers, gaming systems, and so on for every unit each year. However, he could afford to do so for one unit per year. The first year Sam bought that 80" plasma screen we talked about earlier, plus a new espresso station, and a very trendy "classic" gaming system. The condo where he installed these things already had a smaller television, coffee bar, and a gaming system, so Sam took those out and took them to his home to store as backups.

To recap Sam's experience, he owns four condos that he rents on a short-term basis using an app like Airbnb or VRBO. They're available for rent all year, so all of his ordinary and necessary expenses are deductible. He doesn't have to worry about passive activity limitations like Linda, but he does have to pay self-employment tax (FICA X 2) on his profits. Sam rents out his personal residence for 14 days or less, and he doesn't pay tax on - or even report - that income. Sam is able to deduct the cost of travel to see other short-term rentals (as long as it makes good business sense), and he gets to use the section 179 deduction to expense the entire cost of furniture, TVs, gaming systems, etc. he buys for his properties.

Questions for your tax professional:
1. What is bonus depreciation and can I take advantage of it?
2. How can I deduct travel when seeking bigger profits for my short term rental business?
3. What qualifies as long term versus short term rental?
4. How can my family members use my vacation rental without it being treated as my own personal stay?
5. What other benefits (retirement accounts, health insurance deductions, etc) do I get from operating an active short term rental business?
6. How do I determine what is an "ordinary and necessary" expense for a rental property?

How Depreciation Dan makes money from his rental properties

Tax savings potential: $$

Key topics in this story:
Tax
- Depreciation deductions
- Asset appreciation

Business
- Determining rent for different tenants.

If you look at the profit and loss statements for most rental properties, they appear to be losing money. Between mortgage interest, repairs and maintenance, property taxes, insurance premiums, utilities, management fees, and depreciation expense, it looks like owning a rental property is hardly worth the effort involved. How does Dan make money, when on paper he's losing it? Well, let's start by looking at depreciation.

A few years ago our friend Dan bought a rental house. The entire property cost $500,000: a lot for an investment, but the house sits on a good bit of land, and Dan has some future plans for the property. As with any rental property,

Dan takes the purchase price of the property, subtracts the value of the land (because even when the house is used up the land remains), and depreciates the "basis" over 27.5 years. Here's what it looks like:

Purchase price:	$500,000
Value of land:	-$150,000
Depreciable "basis:"	**$350,000**
Depreciation amount:	$350,000 / 27.5 = $12,727

The depreciation of $12,727 is an amount the Dan gets to deduct every year, even though he bought the property in a prior year. In other words, this depreciation "expense" is money Dan didn't spend this year but gets to deduct anyway.

NOTE: Why 27.5 years? There are different periods for all kinds of assets. Rental houses just happen to be 27.5 years. The period for commercial real estate is 39 years, and for a piece of office furniture it's 5 years.

> **Hot Tax Tip**
> Not all expenses equate to cash. When planning for business expenses it makes sense to prioritize the expenses (deductions) that are free.

What is the point of depreciation, anyway? Most pieces of business property wear out over time or become obsolete. Imagine a tool that you buy for your business – in five years it might be trashed or it could be so crappy compared to new tools that it makes sense to chuck it and buy another. The tax code allows you to deduct a part of the price of the tool every year for five years: this is called the depreciation deduction.

But wait, are houses typically worn out and obsolete after 27.5 years? No, not typically, even though the tax code considers them to be a pile of rubble on the day they're fully depreciated. That brings us to the second part of how Dan makes money on his rental property investments: Appreciation. Real estate tends to get more expensive as time goes on, and the $500,000 house Dan bought might be worth $1,000,000 in ten years. We'll cover saving taxes on the sale of a rental property later on, but for now consider that Dan earns cash from rent, gets a tax deduction for money he hasn't spent, and owns an asset that he can sell later on for a lot more than he purchased it for – all while a renter is paying the mortgage!

> **Business Tip**
> A business model typically shows cash in and out, but if your business has other benefits, like appreciation of assets, be sure to include those to make sure you're capturing the complete picture.

Dan owned the rental property we discussed above for ten years, it was a big-time seller's market in his area, and he decided he wanted to unload this property. He called to ask us how much tax he was going to have to pay, and that was a pretty easy answer, generally speaking. "All of it." We told him. "All the taxes. In the world. It's going to be really, really expensive, and we're really glad you called before you finalized anything." If there were ever a time for Dan to talk to his tax professional, that was the time. We went on to describe how much tax Dan was going to have to pay, which breaks down like this:

Most of the tax hit comes from the difference between Dan's basis in the property and the sale price. Let's define those two things in simple terms.

The sale price is the amount Dan received for selling the property, which was $1,000,000. Ok, that one was easy.

The basis is the amount Dan originally spent for the property, minus the depreciation he deducted every year (and some other stuff, but those are the basics).

Michael A. York, EA
Andrew L. Stevens, EA, MBA

Purchase price:	$500,000
Value of land:	$150,000
Depreciable "basis:"	$350,000
Depreciation amount:	$350,000 / 27.5 = $12,727
Years depreciated:	10
Depreciation allowed:	10 years X $12,727 = $127,270
Basis:	$500,000 - $127,270 = $372,730
Taxable gain on sale:	$1,000,000 - $372,730 = **$627,270**

Here's where it gets really painful. The "appreciation" on the investment (the difference between the sale price and the original purchase price) is $500,000. At Dan's long-term capital gains rates (15% for most people), that's $75,000 in taxes (ignoring state income tax for now).

> *Hot Tax Tip*
> Calculating basis can be very tricky, and plenty of things that look like regular expense items actually have a big impact on basis. Talk to a professional tax advisor before you even think of selling an investment property! We feel there are very few "tax traps" in the tax code, but selling a rental property can be one of them. Proceed with caution!

It gets worse. Remember how $127,270 was allowed as a depreciation deduction for 10 years? That amount gets taxed at 25%. The reasoning is this: Dan took a tax deduction for 10 years, which reduced his income and taxes at his regular tax rate. Now he sold the asset, so he has to add back the depreciation he previously deducted, and it gets taxed at a higher rate.

Important Note: You might be thinking, "I know how to get around this: I just won't claim depreciation." The IRS is one step ahead of you: You have pay tax on the depreciation whether you deducted it or not. So, if you really want to imagine someone having a bad day, imagine forgoing a depreciation deduction for 10 years only to find out you have to pay the tax on it anyway. Ouch. (Additional Note: There are ways around this, but you need to talk to a good tax professional to do it correctly and legally. Believe us, you do not want to face a tax bill for this amount plus interest and penalties).

> ### Hot Tax Tip
> Always deduct depreciation if possible. This is one of those pitfalls that tax software doesn't always detect, so put another check in the "pro" column for hiring a professional tax advisor.

Let's continue with Dan's example. At 25%, that means he would pay $31,818 in "depreciation recapture" tax on the $127,270 in depreciation allowable over the years. After wrapping up what he thought was a tidy investment return of $500,000, he now has a tax bill – just on the sale of this property – of $106,818 ($31,818 + $75,000). That's in addition to his other taxes on wages, business income, stock sales, etc. Ouch again.

Many people read Dan's story and say, "But he still made a lot of money! He can easily afford to pay that tax!" Yes, he did, but without proper tax planning it's not uncommon for us to talk to clients who did a deal just like Dan's, and then they reinvested the proceeds and they don't have six figures on hand to pay the tax. If you're not convinced, let's take a look at a second set of numbers to see how Dan's story might have played out if he hadn't sold the property for a big gain.

Many investment properties don't appreciate as much as Dan's did; in fact, many times they appreciate very little. Imagine Dan's rental was purchased for $500,000, but he sold it ten years later for $505,000. In that case Dan's capital gains tax would have been $5k x 15%, or $750, but his tax on the depreciation would still be $31,818! That means he would have "made" $5,000 on the sale of the property, but he would owe $32,568! As we're sure you can imagine, explaining how this works to a client who has fallen into this tax "trap" is one of our least favorite conversations.

Except, Dan's rental property sale might also be tax free. Dan was pretty interested in how to make this a tax-free transaction. Let's look at some of his options below.

Idea #1: He dies. Ok, that's not a great option, but here's how it works: Dan dies and leaves the property to someone. On the date of his death, the basis ($372,730 in the example above) gets "stepped up" to fair market value. In other words, on the day he dies, if the house is worth one million dollars, then his heir's basis in the house is suddenly, magically, one million dollars. If they sell the house the next day for $1,000,001, then their taxable gain is $1,000,001 - $1,000,000, or $1. But, Dan didn't think dying was a good way to avoid taxes, so we told him about some other ideas.

Idea #2: Use a 1031 exchange. There is a provision in the tax code where Dan could "trade" one property for another and avoid (for the time being) paying tax on the gain. A full treatment on the 1031 exchange could make for its own book, so we're not going to go super deep on it here. In summary, Dan wouldn't really be trading one for the other, he would simply follow a bunch of very restrictive parts of the tax code where he would sell one property, identify another to buy within a certain timeframe, and all of the money from the sale of the first property would go into the purchase of the second property. In Dan's case, that would be every cent (or more) of the one million dollars going toward the purchase of the new property (or properties). If the new property needs a new roof, Dan would have to come up with other money to pay for it. Now, 1031 exchanges are great, but they are extremely restrictive, and we're sure you can tell.

Idea #3: Move into the property. This strategy is very tricky, and it takes a few years to implement, so if you want to learn more about it we recommend asking your tax professional.

Idea #4: Invest the proceeds of the sale in a Qualified Opportunity Zone fund. In December 2017 the government rolled out a new law to encourage investment in certain parts of cities, nationwide. In Dan's case, he could take the taxable gain from the sale, $627,270 (or any portion of it) and invest it in the QOZ fund. The rest of the funds from the sale ($372,730) would be his to do with as he pleased.

> ### Don't Go There Doug!
> Doug is doing a 1031 exchange to trade his run-down 8-unit apartment building for a corn field that he plans to convert to an Aussie rules football pitch. Rather than let the intermediaries handle all of the cash, he asked the title company to deliver the check to his office so he could personally make sure it was issued correctly. The check was delivered to his office, and as usual, his assistant deposited the check, thinking it was business income. Don't go there, Doug! By depositing the check, Doug just lost his 1031 tax-deferred status, and he owes tax on the transaction, to the tune of hundreds of thousands of dollars.

> ### Hot Tax Tip
> Real estate is an area that lawmakers focus on when it comes to tax policy. From encouraging home-ownership to benefiting campaign donors, there are often reasons to tweak real estate tax laws, and a good tax pro can help you stay on top of these changes as they happen in real time.

Now, in Dan's case he would still owe tax on the $627,270, but the bill won't come due until the tax year 2026 (payable in April 2027), and depending on how long his money has been in the QOZ fund his tax bill will be reduced by 10%-15%. He still has to pay capital gains tax, but he gets to defer it and reduce it a little. Here's where this gets good:

Dan could take his $627,270 and put it into a QOZ fund, and then direct the fund to purchase a building for $313,635 and put an additional $313,635 into the property in the form of improvements (improvements are required according to the law). Dan could then hold the property for ten years (or more and sell, his tax on that sale would be zero. If he sold after 10 years, whether the property is worth one million or twenty million his tax is zero. If he makes tons of money on the deal, his tax is zero. *NOTE: These QOZ rules are complicated (as you can tell), and we have just hit the tips of the waves when it comes to this strategy. Let's just put it this way: If the people who wrote this law wanted to use it to reduce their tax bill, we would tell them to consult a qualified tax professional to make sure they were doing everything correctly.*

Tell me more about this whole QOZ thing

QOZs are designated low-income tracts where this favorable tax treatment can occur. "Low income" sounds bad, doesn't it? Think of it like this: These are areas the government wants to revitalize, and we'll talk in a second about how they plan to make it happen. This is very new to the tax code as of December, 2017, so if you're hearing about it here for the first time, that's why.

Why would they put this law into effect? It's pretty simple: the government wants private citizens to pour cash into low-income areas in order to create businesses and jobs and help lift these areas out of their low income status. Now, just because these are designated low-income areas does not mean they are necessarily bad investment locations, much like obviously everything in a high-income area isn't necessarily a good investment location. The government is creating a tax strategy to incentivize people to hopefully buy low (in a low-income area) and sell high (once the area is revitalized). We'll talk about how the tax treatment works in detail, but a good general rule is that if the investment in the QOZ property or business is attractive even without the QOZ tax treatment, then it's a good idea to at least investigate it further. Keep that rule in mind as you read on.

> **Business Tip**
> Evaluate investment opportunities first without any tax treatment, and then with all of the tax benefits you hope to receive. If an opportunity looks good with and without tax benefits then it's worth pursuing. If not, extra care and consideration is warranted.

Here's how it works:

Basically, if you have taxable short- or long-term gain on a sale of something (stocks, real estate, etc.) you can delay paying tax on that gain until April of 2027 (the deadline for paying 2026 taxes), as long as you deposit the gain in a QOZ fund within 180 days of the sale. As long as it's the first time being purchased as a QOZ investment, the fund can be used to purchase property, fund a new or existing business that is located in a QOZ, rent space to start a business, or even purchase residential rental property.

There is an obvious benefit to deferring a capital gains tax bill until 2026, but there are some other benefits as well. If the investment is held for five years before 12/31/2026, then the investor gets a 10% discount on the 2026 tax bill. If it's held for seven years before 12/31/2026, the investor gets a 15% discount. If the investment in the QOZ isn't a winner, meaning it's worth less than the gain the investor originally put in, then the tax bill is calculated on the lower amount.

The law stipulates that the investor has to put money into the business or property he or she invests in. They don't want people simply parking their money for a few years and then selling - imagine someone who simply bought an old apartment building, put no money into it, and then sold it and got a tax break. Would that really help the community? Instead, the QOZ fund has to put in an amount equal or greater than the original investment into improvements. Let's use an example. Let's say someone had a $100,000 gain from a stock sale, and they were going to pay tax on it. Instead, they could invest that money in a QOZ fund. The QOZ fund would then be directed to buy a property for $50,000 and put another $50,000 in for improvements.

Michael A. York, EA
Andrew L. Stevens, EA, MBA

Now for the very best part. The investor's tax bill for the previous capital gain will come and go in April 2027, but if the investor continues to hold the property until they have had it for 10 years or more, then when they sell they pay zero tax on the sale. That's right: ZERO TAX!

If all of this is confusing, we get it. It's brand new, there are a lot of what-have-yous, and it could potentially involve a lot of money. Get with a tax professional if you think this might benefit you, or at the very least if you have a big sale of stocks, real estate, a business, or anything else.

Questions for your tax professional:
1. Can you help me calculate the taxable gain if I sold my rental properties?
2. How do estate and tax exclusions impact my estate plan when I leave my rental properties to my heirs?
3. How can I reduce tax on selling a rental property by moving into it?

John, who is doing quite well and wants to invest in a QOZ

Tax savings potential:
$$$$$($$$$$$$$$$$$$$$$$$$$$$$$$$$$$$)

Key topics in this story:
Tax
- Postponing capital gains tax.
- Qualified Opportunity Zones - part of the Tax Cuts & Jobs Act.
- How to pay zero tax on a big windfall.

John is having a great year, because some very smart moves he made in recent years are really paying off. He is about to sell his business, a rental property he owns, some stock he inherited from his grandmother years ago, and some short-term shares in an app company that took off. While John is loving the idea of all of his profits, he is not loving the idea of paying his taxes in April. John's total capital gains are close to $500,000. Broken down, that's $150,000 from the capital gains portion of his business sale, $100,000 in long-term gains from his rental, $50,000 from the shares his grandmother gave him, and $200,000 in short-term gains from his investment in the app.

When estimating John's taxes, we would assume he would pay $60,000 in federal and state taxes on his long-term capital gains, calculated as follows:

Note: This case does not consider certain other taxes that may kick in (AMT, NIIT, et al) for some taxpayers depending on their individual circumstances, such as income phase-outs.

Capital gains from business sale:	$150,000
Rental sale:	$100,000
Inheritance:	$50,000
Total long-term gains:	$300,000
Federal long-term gains tax rate:	15%
Federal long-term gains tax:	$45,000
State long-term gains tax rate (est.):	5%
State long-term gains tax:	$15,000
Total long-term gains tax:	$60,000

John would also pay approximately $84,000 in short-term capital gains tax, calculated as follows:

App investment	$200,000
Fed short-term gains tax rate:	37%
Fed short-term gains tax:	$74,000
State short-term gains tax rate:	5%
State short-term gains tax:	$10,000
Total short-term gains tax:	$84,000

Michael A. York, EA
Andrew L. Stevens, EA, MBA

John's total tax liability on his "great year" is going to be $144,000! While John understands that he is still "up" $356,000, he would love to find a tax strategy that could save him at least some of the $144,000. Later that week while talking with his friends about his tax bill, his friend Mike suggested looking into investing his money in a QOF (qualified opportunity fund) located in a QOZ. John said that he had already looked into a 1031 exchange, but he wanted to get out of real estate, and only his real estate gains would be shielded from tax. Mike explained to John that not all QOF's were real estate investments. For example, Mike had heard of another company that was developing an app that he was going to personally invest in. Mike explained that as long as the QOF business is physically located in the QOZ it qualifies for QOZ treatment, even if it simply rents its business location there and 90% of the assets are held inside of the QOZ (and some other stipulations, talk to your tax pro).

Mike went on to explain an additional benefit of the QOF compared to a 1031 exchange. Whereas with a 1031 exchange all of the proceeds of the sale have to be included, with a QOF investment only the gains need to be invested. This would allow John to keep cash on hand for other investments while taking advantage of one of the most sophisticated tax strategies in the Tax Cuts & Jobs Act, passed in December of 2017.

Let's pull out our crystal ball and look at a possible future scenario for John.

After talking with Mike and the app developers who created their company using a QOF located in a QOZ, John decided to invest his $500,000 of capital gains in the app company. Instead of owing tax on these gains in April, John would be able to delay this tax bill until April of 2027.

If John's money is invested in the fund for 5 years, he gets a discount on his tax bill of 10%. Again, instead of $144,000 due in April, he would owe $129,600 in April of 2027. If John's money is invested for 7 years, he would get a 15% discount on his tax bill, and thus he would owe $122,400 in April of 2027. It should go without saying that in order to get this seven-year, 15% discount the money would need to be invested in the QOF for seven years, thus it would need to be invested by December 31, 2019. In order to get the best advantage for your QOZ investments it makes sense to invest as soon as possible, though the benefits are still great even if you miss the deadlines.

Now, if John's investment in the app company goes bust, and on December 31, 2026 his investment is worth zero, then his tax bill would be zero.

But, let's look deeper into our crystal ball, in a scenario where his investment in the app company pays off big time. In this scenario this app is the next Whatsapp, and after ten years it sells for twenty billion dollars. If you're unfamiliar with Whatsapp, it's an app that was funded with $60M and sold to Facebook for $19B - it was one of the most successful app developments of all time. In any case, let's say John's $500,000 investment pays off for $500,000,000. His tax on that pay out would be... hmmm, what's zero times anything? Oh yeah, zero. Zero tax.

Don't Go There Doug!
Doug wants all of this QOZ tax treatment, so he bought a small building in an qualified opportunity zone and moved his plastic building block "museum & showroom" business into it. Doug didn't consult a tax professional beforehand, and he doesn't realize all of the complications that go along with this strategy. Don't go there, Doug! Anyone seriously considering this strategy should retain a qualified tax professional to make sure they do everything correctly, otherwise the likelihood of losing the tax advantages is high.

Hot Tax Tip
If you have big stock winnings you want to realize but you want to delay paying capital gains tax, the QOZ strategy can be a literal gold mine.

To recap, John was able to delay paying taxes on his gains, and even when the bill came due he got a nice discount for investing in the app company located in the QOZ. When the app company sold and his investment matured, John's tax was zero because he had been invested for over ten years. Let's be clear - this is a tax strategy written into law by and for real estate investors, but as we have said over and over, any tax strategy that is available to anyone else is available to all. Talk to your tax professional to see how this particular strategy can benefit you.

Questions for your tax professional:
1. Do I have taxable gains that could be invested in a QOZ fund?
2. What are the QOZ areas that I can invest in?
3. What is 1202 stock, and how can I benefit from it?
4. What deadlines related to QOZ investing have I missed, and what options are still available to me?

Mobile the Notary Mary

Tax savings potential: $$$

Key topics in this story:
Tax
- The home office - a real world example.
- Automobiles - SUV vs electric.
- Continuing education deductions.
- Deducting your cruise ship travel.

Business
- Spotting opportunities among service providers you meet.
- Common barriers to entry.
- Dealmaking.
- Referrals - the best way to grow your business.
- How to protect yourself when you're selling your own time.

Mary worked as a dental hygienist and was looking for a way to make extra income on her days off. She and her husband had recently bought a house, and when they signed the closing documents they were delayed for about 30 minutes as they waited for the mobile notary, Karyn, to arrive. When Karyn did finally arrive, she was rushed and out of breath, and apologized for being late. She admitted to being incredibly busy, and she confessed that she needed to hire people to take some work off her hands. A light bulb went off in Mary's head. She took the card from the notary, and the next week she gave her a call.

In the meantime, Mary applied to become a notary and passed the tests required by her state. When she spoke to Karyn, she proposed a deal: Mary would open her own mobile notary business. She and Karyn would refer business to each other when they were too busy to take a job, and they would charge each other a referral fee for doing so. Karyn agreed because this would allow her to make money from referrals and not have to hire employees and all the headaches that can come along with managing them.

On her days off from dental hygiene, Mary charges $40 per notary visit (check local laws) and she typically does about seven visits per day.

Let's look at how this business works and how Mary got into it.

Mary was actively looking for a way to make extra income aside from her normal employment, and when she saw how busy her mobile notary was, it occurred to her that this was a field that needed more service providers. It's not always so easy to spot opportunities, but there are always signs. If you see an overworked service provider, it's a sign that there is pent up demand that they are struggling to fill. If you experience bad customer service, it's a sign that there are limited choices for consumers. And if you feel like the amount of money you're paying for something is way out of whack for what you're receiving, then there is space for additional suppliers to enter the market and compete for customers.

Once the opportunity was identified, Mary needed to figure out how to get involved in the business and make some deals. With any new business there are barriers to entry, which basically means there are things that established companies have that new companies need to build or buy in order to compete. It's a pretty simple concept: typical barriers are investment in property, real estate, equipment, and people. Government regulation can be a barrier as well. There can also be economies of scale, distribution and supply networks, and response from competitors, but we will discuss those later on. Luckily the barriers to entry for Mary's business were small, but let's go over them anyway.

> *Business Tip*
> Analyzing barriers to entry can help you decide whether a new business is worth pursuing, but it can also help you understand your existing business better.

A mobile notary needs to have reliable transportation (investment in equipment), a notary license (regulation), and time to perform services (investment in people). These are small barriers compared to, say, starting a major airline. She already had the car and she was looking for a way to spend her free time making extra money, so her main barrier was the notary license. In her state she was required to pass a test, post a bond, and order some supplies, and once that was all finished she was free to pursue clients.

Next, let's look at the deal Mary made. She approached Karyn with a plan already in mind. It's always helpful to have your side of any deal mapped out before you talk to anyone, otherwise you may agree to terms that are very beneficial to the other side without addressing the key points on your side. To be clear, it's ok to agree to terms that are beneficial to the other side. Deals should never be one-sided, otherwise you run the risk of the other side defaulting, going out of business, or choosing to go to court rather than honoring the deal. Think of it as a way for each side to build their business, rather than approaching it as a battleground. In any case, you need to fully understand your needs before you begin the process. Mary did that by studying her prospective business, knowing what she wanted from Karyn, and knowing what she would be comfortable giving up in return.

>
>
> *Business Tip*
> Making deals is an art and a science, and the more you do it the better you will become. Running your own business will give you ample opportunities to find and complete deals, which is invaluable experience no matter where your career takes you.

Mary also understood that it would benefit Karyn to do a deal. Think about it - Karyn couldn't prevent Mary from starting her business (not legally anyway), so Karyn had two options: 1) Mary goes into business and Karyn gets no benefit at all, or 2) Mary goes into business and Karyn agrees to a deal where they give each other a referral fee. In a situation like this it's always a good idea to talk to an attorney beforehand, because there are ways arrangements like these can run afoul of the law. It should be a quick chat and it shouldn't cost too much money.

The main point of this deal was about referrals, which is one of the most powerful concepts for any business. A referral is simply one person recommending a business to another. Referrals can be simply word-of-mouth between people, or they can be very formalized structures like when a doctor sends a patient to a specialist for a more in-depth examination. Any time you've told a friend about your new favorite restaurant you've made a referral. Many businesses get the majority of their clientele from referrals, and before search engines put everything at our fingertips, there were really two types of businesses: those that paid for big ad campaigns, and those that survived on referrals.

>
>
> *Business Tip*
> The cheapest and best way to build a business is through referrals. The hardest part of getting referrals is to ask for them. Get used to asking for referrals: the sooner the better!

That leads us to another important point. Eventually Mary was able to build a website to represent her business, but that took a little time. It took even more time for search engines to "crawl" her website and to have it show up in search results and even then she wasn't on the all-important first page. It took even longer to get that first page ranking. The referral deal with Karyn allowed Mary to start servicing clients almost immediately, which provided cash to pay a web developer. Mary could have invested her own money in her website, but isn't it better to let the business pay for it?

Mary's website is first class. In a business like hers (and many, many others), the website is the first and most important marketing tool: It's the basis of every client's first impression, it communicates professionalism, and it contains critical information clients need to make a hiring decision. Mary could have built the website herself using one of many free templates online. Instead, she hired a professional to ensure that it would fit her business perfectly, and so she could rely on the professional's knowledge of current search engine optimization (SEO) tactics. Not every business needs a custom-built website. If your main source of advertising is online search, and your main method of communicating to new customers is your website, it makes sense to at least consult a professional.

As a service provider who meets with clients on a set schedule, Mary sold time, which is a tricky thing that deserves some discussion. Ultimately, Mary's service was limited by the hours in the day and the hours she could devote to serving customers. In a business like this, it's important to get paid in advance if you can. Let's talk about why: If you have, say, five hours to work and you can make one appointment per hour, that's five possible appointments. If you miss an appointment you can never make it up unless you add hours to your working time (and in some cases that's not possible). If someone flakes on you, that is the same thing as agreeing to purchase a product, then lighting it on fire, and then refusing to pay for it. In other words, once an hour passes you can never re-sell it. Unlike physical goods that can sit on a shelf indefinitely, we can never stockpile and resell time.

Think about a ball game where you have to pay for your ticket in advance (before walking into the stadium). There are two key reasons why it works that way. The purpose of an advance ticket is to guarantee a seat for the purchaser, but from the team owner's perspective it's to make sure the reservation is paid for even if the ticket-holder decides not to show up. After all, the players still play the game (and get paid for it) whether the fans stay home or not. It works the same way when you sell your own time: if you have an 11:00 am appointment to service a client and they decide to flake out at 10:55 am, you can't sell that time to someone else. It's totally possible that you turned away other business once you blocked off that time slot. If that's the case in your business, your goal should be to get paid in advance.

No one likes paying in advance, and no one likes "no cancellation" policies. Here are some work-arounds. One, arrange to accept a deposit instead of taking full payment. Paying a deposit is more palatable to consumers than paying in full up-front, and it will provide you some measure of protection when people cancel at the last minute. Another solution is to take a credit card number in advance, but only charge it once the job is done, or if the appointment is cancelled within a specified period of time (such as 48 hours before the scheduled appointment). Offering to reschedule an appointment that is canceled at the last minute doesn't help much, because you're basically getting paid once for two appointment slots.

> Business Tip
> If you ever give a refund to someone who paid with a credit card, only issue the refund to that same credit card. If you give a refund via cash, the customer can still request a "chargeback," which you will likely lose, and you will be out the cash and the credit card chargeback, plus fees.

Our favorite technique that we've seen is to offer "cancellation protection." Here's how it works: All appointments are paid for in advance, but clients can choose to purchase the ability to cancel or reschedule for a modest sum, say 5-10% of the price. It's a voluntary add-on for the consumer, and plenty of people will say, "No, that's ok, I'm not going to need to reschedule." However, plenty of people will opt to purchase the add-on, which is a nice additional little cash flow. Here's where it gets good: When someone cancels and asks for their money back you simply check to see if they purchased cancellation protection. If they did, no problem, you refund their money and keep the amount they paid for the cancellation protection. If they didn't, now you have a great rebuttal: "I'm sorry, when you set up the appointment you said you wouldn't need to cancel, and you chose not to add the cancellation protection. I'm afraid there's nothing I can do…"

You might still decide that it's best for business to offer refunds to people who cancel, but you should strongly consider what it means to your bottom line when your time that you thought was bought and paid for suddenly is wasted. You can't get it back.

Mary runs her business out of her home, and she maintains an office where she makes appointments, plans out her day, takes calls, and responds to emails and other messages. Contrary to an opinion we hear very frequently, an office in the home is not an automatic audit trigger, and it isn't overly risky. It's a mainstay of the tax code, it's completely necessary for many people's businesses, and there is nothing wrong with taking an appropriate tax deduction. Let's look at the rules.

First, the office in the home must be used regularly and exclusively for business. If Mary's home office doubled as her toddler's play area, that wouldn't be an exclusive use. Likewise, if she only used the office occasionally because she had another office elsewhere, that also wouldn't necessarily qualify. Mary didn't have a totally separate room to use for business, so she bought a room divider (which was tax deductible) and used it to create a work area that was separate from her personal space.

Second, the office must be either the principal place of business, a place to meet clients or customers, or a separate structure not attached to the home, like a garage or shed. Mary's office was attached to her home, and she didn't meet clients there, but it was her principal place of business in the sense that every other "place" where she conducted her mobile notary trade was a different location every time. In other words, she had dozens of temporary places where she notarized forms, and one principal place where she conducted her administrative and management duties: her home office.

Don't Go There Doug!

Doug runs a business, and he has an office at his company with a desk, computer, and a sign on the door with his name on it. Like many of us, he brings work home with him, and he often does his work sitting on the couch in front of the TV while watching whatever his kids force him to watch. Occasionally, he can sneak off and use his dining table as a work area, and sometimes (almost every night) he works while reclining in his bed. His company deducts his home office expenses through an accountable plan, including his couch, dining table, and bed. Don't go there, Doug! If you already have an office, then your home office probably isn't your "principal place of business." Now, if Doug meets clients in his home office or if the office is a separate structure from his house, that's a different story. Simply doing work from home doesn't qualify for a home office deduction, and things like the living room couch, dining room table, and sleeping quarters are pretty much never deductible home office expenses.

Hot Tax Tip

Mary used the square footage method to calculate her home office deduction, but there are two other methods. Use the one that provides the biggest deduction.

Michael A. York, EA
Andrew L. Stevens, EA, MBA

Mary measured the square footage of her home office and figured out the percentage of her home that her office occupies. She applies that percentage to her mortgage interest, property taxes, utilities (including wifi), and other house-related expenses and deducts those from her business income.

Of course, one of Mary's biggest expenses is her vehicle. She often drives over fifty miles per day, and she is constantly in her car going from appointment to appointment. Mary uses an app to log her business miles, and she tracks all of her expenses very closely: gasoline purchases, maintenance costs, tires, tolls, taxes, state fees, etc. It's a common misconception that if you deduct actual expenses rather than mileage, you don't need to keep track of miles. In reality, even if you choose to deduct actual expenses you still can only deduct the business percentage of those expenses, which is calculated using mileage.

After a year of running her business Mary decided that it made business sense to purchase a separate, energy efficient vehicle that would be used exclusively for her mobile notary business. Around mid-December Mary was looking at her results from the year, and she realized that her personal vehicle was getting more wear and tear than she would have liked, and that a more economical vehicle would allow her to operate more efficiently. She first looked at SUVs, which sometimes have a pretty impressive benefit. SUVs that weigh more than 6,000 pounds of gross vehicle weight (an easily researchable figure) qualify for a 100% "bonus" depreciation expense in the first year. Of course, you can only use the business use percentage of any vehicle, but in Mary's case this was a vehicle that she bought for business and no other purpose, and she had a personal vehicle she used when not conducting business.

Let's look at one of the vehicles she considered:

A new luxury SUV starts at about $60,000. If 100% used for business, that means Mary could deduct $60,000 in the first year, even if she financed the vehicle! If she bought a used SUV that met the 6,000 lb. gross vehicle weight restriction, she could deduct 100% of the cost of that vehicle as well. That is a major deduction, but after looking at the particulars of her business and the cost to maintain and drive an SUV, Mary decided that she didn't need a big vehicle, and the extra costs due to gasoline, tires, insurance, and maintenance compared to a small car were not going to help her business be profitable given the amount of miles Mary drove.

Next, Mary looked at electric vehicles, which she liked because of the environmental benefits, not to mention the affordable cost of operating and maintaining one. She found that depending on the vehicle, whether it's all electric, or gas-electric hybrid, and some other factors, she could get a tax credit up to $7,500. Whereas deductions lower your income, tax credits lower your actual taxes. In other words, if Mary bought an electric vehicle, and her actual tax bill at the end of the year was $7,500 or less, then her electric vehicle credit would wipe out her tax bill and she would end up paying zero taxes for the year.

> *Hot Tax Tip*
> These tax credits change from time to time, and they're different for each vehicle, so be sure to check the latest figures before making a purchase decision, and of course always talk to your tax professional.

Mary purchased her electric vehicle in late December. In addition to the $7,500 credit, Mary could still depreciate the vehicle over five years, and still deduct all of her expenses for operating it. She continued to track all of her miles in order to prove that her use was 100% business, and she made sure to link her toll tag to her business bank account for this vehicle.

One question Mary was sometimes asked is how her vehicle could be 100% business use if she traveled to and from home every day. Commuting is never deductible, but because Mary's morning commute was from the kitchen where she had coffee and breakfast to her home office, then every trip afterward was deductible. Likewise, her final trip home every day wasn't commuting, because her work day wasn't over until she visited her home office to send out reminders and answer emails. Thus, her commute at the end of the day was from her office to her living room, where she often plopped onto the couch with a book (like this one?) and a glass of wine when her work day was finally finished.

You might think that Mary's continuing education needs would be pretty light with a business like this one. After all, most states don't require CPE credits to maintain a notary license. However, the key to remember with continuing education is that it doesn't have to be specifically for the principal product or service a business provides. Every year Mary picks a business topic that she would like to improve, and she finds a seminar where she can learn more about that topic and network with experts. Last year Mary decided that she wanted to know more about web development and how it could apply to her business, so she could take more control over her website's look and feel, and so she would know if her web developer was shooting her straight with the effort required for various improvements. Mary is not in the web development business, but her business has a website, so she can deduct the expense of traveling to learn more about how to manage it. In this case, Mary found a class being offered on a cruise ship.

The law allows a deduction of up to $2,000 for attending a seminar on a cruise ship, with a few restrictions: The boat has to fly under an American flag, the ports-of-call all need to be in the U.S. or its possessions, and you must attach statements to your tax return from yourself and an officer of the organization sponsoring the seminar showing the schedule of events and how much time you spent at the scheduled business activities. Mary documented appropriately and got a nice deduction for learning some great material, meeting helpful people, and spending several days on a luxury cruise ship. It was practically a vacation, even though it was demonstrably a business trip. Not bad at all, Mary.

> *Hot Tax Tip*
> When it comes to business travel, cruises are among the most restrictive in terms of record keeping and destinations available. However, if you really want your cruise to be a business trip it can be done (with your tax pro's help).

To recap, Mary found an opportunity to start her own business, and she networked with other business people in her town to identify customers for a small referral fee. Mary used funds from her business to invest in a first-rate website, and she carefully considered the ramifications of selling time, rather than selling goods. Mary took advantage of the office in the home deduction, and she consulted with her tax professional to choose a vehicle that was appropriate for her business, but also gave her a nice tax break. Finally, even though her primary service doesn't require continuing education, as a business owner Mary is entitled to deduct any educational seminar or activity that improves her business. For at least one year, she followed the rules that enabled her to take a big deduction for spending several days on a luxury cruise ship.

Questions for your tax professional:
1. Is my home office set up correctly to be regularly and exclusively used for business?
2. How does "principal place of business" apply to my home office?
3. What documentation should I maintain to support my home office deduction?
4. Which method of calculating my home office deduction is most advantageous to me?
5. Would I benefit from buying a business-only vehicle?
6. Can I take a cruise and deduct it as a business expense?
7. What entity should I choose for my business?

Business travel: Everyone's a winner!

There are a few expense categories that tend to be "big ticket" items compared to other things, like medical expenses, vehicle expenses, and travel expenses. Those are the categories where we should look for tax deductions, because they tend to yield the biggest savings for the effort involved. If we called you up and said, "Great news! We found a way to deduct 100% of your annual budget for paper clips." You would probably say, "Is that great news? It sounds like small to extra-small news at best." On the other hand, if we told you that you could legally deduct your out-of-pocket medical expenses, wouldn't that be great? If you're interested, read about Yolanda and her Medical Reimbursement Plan, which are discussed in their own story elsewhere in this book. Likewise, if you want to learn how to deduct your travel expenses, read on.

Michael A. York, EA
Andrew L. Stevens, EA, MBA

Javier, whose business takes him to some amazing places

Tax savings potential: $$$$

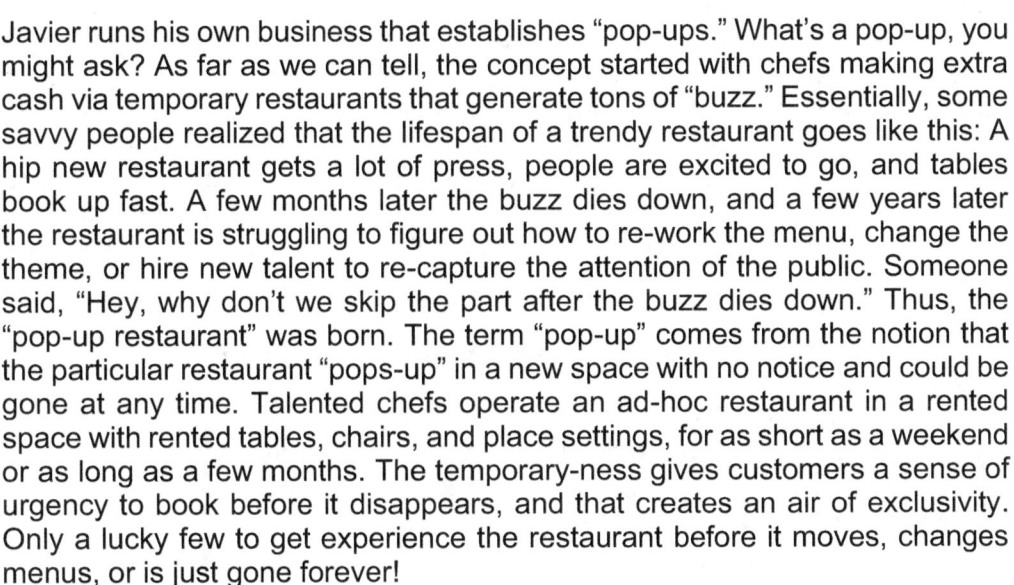

Key topics in this story:
Tax
- Business travel: All the rules.

Business
- Why a "pop-up" business?

Javier runs his own business that establishes "pop-ups." What's a pop-up, you might ask? As far as we can tell, the concept started with chefs making extra cash via temporary restaurants that generate tons of "buzz." Essentially, some savvy people realized that the lifespan of a trendy restaurant goes like this: A hip new restaurant gets a lot of press, people are excited to go, and tables book up fast. A few months later the buzz dies down, and a few years later the restaurant is struggling to figure out how to re-work the menu, change the theme, or hire new talent to re-capture the attention of the public. Someone said, "Hey, why don't we skip the part after the buzz dies down." Thus, the "pop-up restaurant" was born. The term "pop-up" comes from the notion that the particular restaurant "pops-up" in a new space with no notice and could be gone at any time. Talented chefs operate an ad-hoc restaurant in a rented space with rented tables, chairs, and place settings, for as short as a weekend or as long as a few months. The temporary-ness gives customers a sense of urgency to book before it disappears, and that creates an air of exclusivity. Only a lucky few to get experience the restaurant before it moves, changes menus, or is just gone forever!

> ### *Business Tip*
> If we're being cynical, we might point out that a benefit of a pop-up is that permitting is often ignored, and the business is gone right around the time the regulators start to notice that the space isn't up to code. But, we're not usually that cynical.

Creative business people expanded the concept to other activities beyond restaurants, and there are pop-up Instagram portrait studios, toy chests, and Javier's business, which is a place for classic board games. Customers reserve spots online or in-person to play games like Risk, Stratego, Life, Monopoly, Scrabble, Checkers, and more. Tickets are purchased by the hour, and customers tend to spend between one to four hours playing games with new friends and snacking on food and drinks they bring with them. Javier tends to move his business to a new neighborhood every six months or so, which is when the novelty wears off and business slows down. Occasionally Javier considers moving to a new city.

Javier is very careful about when and where he moves his business, and the way he travels to find new locations is very tax advantageous. Now, you might be thinking that all Javier has to do is claim that he's location-scouting and he can deduct any trip he takes, but that's not necessarily true. ("Profit motive" and "ordinary and necessary" are the governing terms, so it's not like Javier can simply claim that every trip he takes is a business expense). Deducting business travel isn't quite that easy, but the way Javier does it can be applied to just about anyone who runs a business. Let's walk through some rules and examples.

> ### *Don't Go There Doug!*
> Doug takes a "business" trip every year, usually to a sunny, tropical destination where he relaxes on the beach all day. Doug tries to claim his trip as a business deduction because his sun hat has his company's logo on it and he usually talks to at least one person in the hot tub about his business. Don't go there, Doug! Doug is not preplanning his hot tub meetings, nor is his sun hat providing any real advertising. Don't be like Doug. Talk with a tax professional to learn how to properly deduct your business travel!

Michael A. York, EA
Andrew L. Stevens, EA, MBA

First, the rules: In order to be deductible, business travel needs to meet three tests:

1. There must be a business reason for the travel
2. It must be pre-planned
3. It must be majority business

Let's see how those apply to Javier. There are a few reasons for business travel the IRS will accept, and as we said, location scouting is not one of them unless it fits with the business model (profit motive) and it's ordinary and necessary in the business. We would argue that location scouting is a key part of Javier's business, but his is a rare exception. Moreover, it wouldn't make business sense for Javier to take more than one or two location scouting trips per year. Why not? Because business travel is expensive, and such large expenses eat away at profits. The IRS knows that if you are running a business to make money, you're not going to blow all that money on lavish trips that don't have a direct effect on adding revenue.

For most other businesses, meeting with a potential client or supplier will count as an acceptable reason for business travel. For virtually any business, education is an undeniable reason to deduct the cost of business travel. Let's look into that: Education is a broad concept, and typically people think of attending classes or seminars when they think of business education. What many people don't know is that education can also mean having a one-on-one with another business person in order to receive coaching or simply to share information, and it's not necessary to pay that other person(s) for their time. Thus, while Javier can't necessarily say he's simply scouting locations for every new city he visits, what he can do is meet with other pop-up owners in those cities and share information with them. That information can help him improve his business, cut costs, and find new revenue streams. It should go without saying that Javier can combine reasons for business travel, such as meeting with potential clients and attending educational meetings on the same trip.

> *Records Check*
> Documenting a reason for business travel is essential. It also needs to make business sense. Be sure to capture the reason for the travel, and the way it impacts your ability to make money.

Seminars and classes don't necessarily need to be in your field in order to be valid for your business. Any major corporation in America has all kinds of functions. They have HR, marketing, tax, treasury, strategic planning, business development, sales, customer experience, and so on. When you run a small business, all of the tasks performed by all of those departments have to be performed by you and your team. Thus, just because Javier runs a board gaming pop-up doesn't mean he wouldn't benefit from traveling to take a seminar on HR compliance.

> *Records Check*
> Business travel must be pre-planned, so get in touch with your suppliers, customers, or industry contacts ahead of time and be sure to save those emails!

The next rule is that business travel must be pre-planned. In other words, if you're on a trip and you meet up with another business person by happenstance, that doesn't magically make your trip deductible as a business expense. We're sure you can imagine why the IRS is hip to such a claim: "There I was, on the golf course in Orlando, when wouldn't you know it, another guy in my foursome was also in business, and we talked non-stop the whole 18 holes. So, yeah, of course it was a business trip!" Pre-planning business travel is as easy as sending an email to a contact letting them know you look forward to meeting them. You simply need dated evidence prior to the trip showing the intended purpose and a valid business reason for the travel.

> ### Records Check
> An hour-by-hour calendar of your business travel, with the names of your contacts, how long you spent doing each activity, and the business purpose behind each activity will help substantiate the business percentage of each day.

Finally, the majority of the trip needs to be about business, and we divide the trip between business days and non-business days. For a trip to be a deductible business trip, including airfare and travel expenses, then most of the days of the trip need to be "business days." If you go on a seven-day trip and only conduct business two out of those seven days, then you can probably deduct the portion of your expenses that are related to those two days, but the rest of the trip is not deductible, including your airfare and other travel expenses. However, there are some "tricks" you can use. Travel days count as business days, so if you take a flight or drive more than 300 miles that counts as a business day. Likewise, weekends count as business days if you conduct business on Friday and Monday with the weekend in-between.

Let's walk through one of Javier's trips. First, he identifies a city where he might want to move one of his pop-ups. He researches other pop-ups in the city and reaches out to the owners of those businesses. He finds a few of them who have time to meet, and he arranges those meetings, usually to be held over coffee or lunch. Next, he books his airfare and hotels or Airbnb, and he typically spends a week or so in a given city.

When it's time for the trip, this is how it typically goes down: He flies in on a Thursday, usually in the morning. Thursday is a travel day, so the rest of the day is his to do as he pleases, but it still counts as a business day. On Friday, Javier meets with a contact and he learns what he can about pop-ups in the area. He also shares information on his home city, and when he finishes that meeting his network is larger and he has been educated on the local market. Later in the day he might drive around using a commercial real estate app to scout locations, or he might meet with a real estate agent. With all of this activity, Friday is clearly a business day, and he has the evening free to do as he pleases. (Note: A single meeting over coffee or lunch probably won't justify counting Friday as a business day). On Saturday and Sunday, Javier is free to do as he pleases, and since these are weekend days they count as business days. If you're keeping score: Javier has had most of Thursday, a part of Friday, and all of Saturday and Sunday to engage in whatever he wants, and yet those are all still considered business days. Monday rolls around and Javier meets with another pop-up owner and a potential landlord. Javier takes Tuesday as a personal day and he conducts no business. Wednesday he flies home in the late afternoon after spending most of the day doing personal activities. When all is said and done, Javier accumulated six out of seven business days for his trip (two travel days, two weekend days, and two days where he conducted business), and thus the entire cost of his airfare, hotel, rental car, meal per diem, and other necessary expenses are tax deductible.

You might be wondering: "But I don't have a business with a location that changes, so how can I deduct my business travel?" It's easy! You simply do what Javier did: Pre-plan the business part of your trip, make sure the majority of your trip is business, and have a valid business reason for your trip. That last one is where most people get hung up, but it's also easy to solve. If you can meet with a potential client or supplier, or engage in educational activities (seminars, classes, or one-on-one coaching or information sharing sessions), you have a valid business purpose.

> ### Records Check
> Don't even think about deducting a hotel room unless you save the receipt. If you didn't save the receipt, call the hotel and get them to email you one.

One last point about Javier and his business travels concerns records retention. Hotel receipts are important to save, because the IRS knows you can pack several people into a hotel room, and the cost of your friends' stay is not tax deductible as a business expense. The receipt from the hotel shows the occupancy of the room, and without it you can't prove that you aren't deducting a trip with your buddies as a "business" expense. Likewise, even though your credit card statement might show that you spent $200 at the office supply store, the IRS knows that they sell video games and snacks at those places in addition to calendars and notepads. Plenty of retailers will email a receipt to you, and it's easy enough to simply archive those emails and retrieve them when you need them. Otherwise, at the very least just stuff them in an envelope at the end of every day, and clearly record the date range on the envelopes when they fill up, otherwise in two years if you get audited you are going to be digging through a lot of receipts looking for what you need.

Questions for your tax professional:
1. What are valid reasons for business travel and how can I document them in my business?
2. Should I count on using the per diem allowance for meals or save receipts?
3. What can I deduct if I don't meet the requirements to make the entire trip a "business" trip?

Hockey Mom Cassandra is on the road

Tax savings potential: $$$$

Key topics in this story:
Tax

- Business travel with a friend or family member.
- Frequent non-deductible trips - how to find a way to make them deductible.

Cassandra's son Isaac is a very good hockey player, and he plays for a traveling team that spends many weekends playing in tournaments all over the country. As you can imagine, Cassandra spends a fortune hauling her son and his stinky gear around the country. To make things worse, it seems like every tournament features some piece of lost or broken equipment as its most memorable moment. Cassandra had an idea: she went to her local hockey equipment retailer and spoke to them about repping hockey equipment at the tournaments. They suggested she contact the regional salesman for one of the hockey stick manufacturers, which she did. The regional salesman helped her get set up with a banner, some merchandise, and some promotional materials. She purchased a collapsible booth on her own.

> ### Don't go there Doug!
> Doug goes to dog shows, and he claims that they are business trips because he sells special copper dog collars through an online storefront. He doesn't set up a booth, he doesn't arrange meetings or training beforehand, and if someone does manage to ask about collars, he simply points them to his website. Don't go there, Doug! Business trips are about conducting business, and they need to be organized as such.

Before setting off to a tournament with her son, Cassandra first contacts the venue to get permission to set up her booth (pre-planning the business purpose of the trip in the process). Once they arrive her son heads off with the team, and she sets up her booth to sell sticks, tape, gloves, and other gear to the parents of other players. She can't work all day without a break, so she usually closes the booth right about the time her son's game is about to start, and she re-opens about the time the game is finished. Cassandra makes a pretty impressive amount of money, and because she has a profit motive and follows the rules (pre-planning, business purpose, majority business), she can deduct the cost of traveling with her son to his hockey tournaments.

Want to make this strategy even better? Take a look at the story "Leigh and Cassy's Handmade Mugs" a little later in the book. If she structured things correctly, Cassandra could potentially hire her son to work in her business, and that would make his travel expenses deductible, too!

Records Check
Cassandra pays for a double occupancy room, but because her son isn't conducting business his stay isn't deductible, so Cassandra is limited to deducting the single occupancy rate.

Questions for your tax professional:
1. What are valid reasons for business travel and how can I document them in my business?
2. Should I count on using the per diem allowance for meals or save receipts?
3. What can I deduct if I don't meet the requirements to make the entire trip a "business" trip?
4. What portion of my business travel can I deduct if my friend or family travels with me?

Timothy travels internationally for business

Tax savings potential: $$$

Key topics in this story:
Tax
- International travel - how is it different from domestic travel for tax purposes?
- International travel - what are the specific rules?

Business
- How to calculate whether the hassle of all this tax stuff is worth it.

Timothy caught the travel bug when he was young, and he literally counts the days between flights out of the country. He operates a channel on a popular video site that features international dishes, and he sells clothing, souvenirs, and spices he brings home from his travels. For example, from a recent trip to India, he brought home a bolt of fabric to make sarongs, some trinkets, and a mountain of Indian spices. His site featured photography of the cooking process in India with an impressive write-up, plus an "Americanized" version of the recipe, and the ability to make the experience really authentic by buying Timothy's spices and Indian souvenirs.

The rules for international business travel are a bit different from regular business travel. Unlike regular business travel, where it's common to pro-rate expenses between business and personal accounts, international travel can be 100% deductible if any of the following "tests" are met. Just pass one of these tests and 100% of the trip is deductible, as long as the three previous rules are met: a. there is a business purpose, b. the trip is pre-planned, and c. it is majority business. (Note: You can still pro-rate the trip between business days and non-business days if you can't pass any of the tests below.)

1. You don't have substantial control over the planning of the trip. If you're running your own business, and traveling internationally for business reasons, this test is going to be difficult to pass. This test is more applicable to people who work for someone who sends them on an international trip. If you're a contractor working on a 1099, and your boss plans your trip, it's probably 100% deductible.

2. You're outside the US for less than a week. For some reason, the day you depart the US doesn't count, but the day you come home does. In other words, the day you fly out of the US counts as a day in the US, and the day you fly home counts as a day in a foreign country. If you fly out on a Monday and fly home on the following Sunday, that's six days abroad, and thus your business trip is entirely deductible.
3. You spend more than 75% of your time on business related activities. We're talking taxes here, where you have to prove that you're innocent, so this test is tougher to meet than it sounds. You have to have pretty strong documentation to show that you spent more than 75% of your waking hours on business. However, both flights count as business time, as does traveling between meetings. If you can keep a written record of your time, backed up with receipts, meeting notes, and other documentation, you can pass this test and deduct 100% of your international travel.
4. Prove that a vacation wasn't a "major consideration" of the trip. In other words, if you spend one day touring Paris and the next with your family at EuroDisney, the IRS isn't likely to let you pass this test.

Don't Go There Doug!

Doug booked an international business trip to Europe, accompanied by his assistant. It's a short trip, just a few nights in Paris and a quick train ride to spend the night in Bruges before flying home, so he thinks it qualifies for #2 above. Doug doesn't schedule any business meetings, and he doesn't take any training or gain any education, but he occasionally has a business idea as he sight-sees with his assistant, who is also his significant other. He claims that his trip is over 75% business because he's with his assistant 24 hours per day, doing business stuff. His assistant shares a room with him in order to save costs, and the assistant's duties include making sure Doug isn't late for things, that he's dressed appropriately, and taking notes when Doug has his business brainstorms. Don't go there, Doug! Simply put, if you can see the problems with this one, so can the IRS.

So how does Timothy navigate these rules? For starters he pre-plans his trips just like regular business travel. He researches where he can go, what he can do, and what he can film and learn ahead of time, and he contacts people and arranges to meet them before he buys his airfare and reserves his hotel rooms. Once he's in-country, his channel becomes his part of his documentation that 75% of his time was spent on business activities, in the form of daily reports of what he did, who he met, what he learned, and what viewers can expect when he brings home inventory and posts full recipes. He takes lots of photographs and video and posts those, too. He also keeps a day planner on his smartphone, where he records where he was, the business purpose, and the time spent on the activity. Naturally he also saves receipts, hotel bills, train and bus tickets, and every other scrap of documentation from the trip.

> ### Records Check
> Timothy keeps a folder for each trip where he stores all of his receipts and other documentation. He travels with the folder, fills it up, and when he comes home it gets stored with his other tax data. He also uses his phone to take pictures of all of his receipts and the end of every day.

If all of this sounds like a fair amount of work to go through to take a deduction for a business trip, you're right. However, think for a second about how much you would want to be paid per hour to do things like document your own activities for a few days, then calculate the cost of a trip abroad. If your hourly rate is less than the tax savings for documenting your business trip appropriately then it makes sense to add the "hassle factor" to your life and take the deductions you have earned.

Questions for your tax professional:
1. What is considered international business travel (e.g. US Virgin Islands)?
2. What are valid reasons for business travel and how can I document them in my business?
3. Should I count on using the per diem allowance for meals or save receipts?
4. What can I deduct if I don't meet the requirements to make the entire trip a "business" trip?
5. What portion of my business travel can I deduct if my friend or family travels with me?
6. How do the tests for deducting 100% of business travel apply to me?

Tom adds up his annual business income like everyone else and it's costing him money

Tax savings potential: $$$

Key topics in this story:
Tax
- Not all deposits are income.
- Cash vs Accrual basis: what's the big deal?

Business
- Should I use a bookkeeping app?

Tom has a business running a landscaping company, and his clients pay him via an app that lets them deposit money in his business bank account. Every January, Tom simply totals his deposits and writes that down as his income when preparing to file his tax return. We bet that sounds familiar to a lot of people.

Here's the problem: Not every deposit is income. The time when Tom returned a tool to the home improvement store and they put the refund back on his debit card looks like income at the end of the year. The few instances where his business account was a little short to pay bills and Tom transferred some personal money into the account: those look like income at the end of the year, too. Or if Tom had put down a security deposit when renting a tool or a vehicle, and that deposit was returned, that looks like income if you simply add up deposits. Sometimes the bank will refund a charge, or Tom might cancel a pre-paid service contract and get a refund for that, and any number of other things might happen that take the form of deposits in his bank account. However, those things aren't necessarily taxable income.

> *Hot Tax Tip*
> If you are calculating your total revenue based on your deposits, you are almost certainly overpaying your taxes.

> *Records Check*
> If you're not accurately documenting deposits in your bank account, the IRS will be happy to classify them all as income.

The best thing to do is to use a service that lets you review all of your bank transactions and code them appropriately in real time. Nine months after the fact, it's impossible to simply see a number and remember exactly what it was related to, but in real time you can pick off non-revenue deposits and save real money.

What do we mean "in real time?" Allow us to explain. There are plenty of bookkeeping software packages out there, and there is surely one that meets your budget and has the features you need. For most businesses, all you really need is something that interfaces with your bank account and lets you "code" transactions. You log in periodically and select from a drop-down menu the appropriate choice for each expense or deposit. Most applications will "learn" what each selection is over time. For example, if every month you pay a subcontractor, your software will learn that this monthly payment is for subcontractors, and you won't have to code that transaction every month, just review it. The point is, tracking this stuff using software takes about 10 minutes per week, even if you have a lot of transactions. It even feels good to do it, probably how our great-grandparents felt back when people used to balance their checkbooks.

These days Tom uses an online bookkeeping app to track his income and expenses (a bookkeeper could do the same thing, but in Tom's case he uses an app), but there is a possibility he set it up incorrectly from the beginning, and that could cost him money. Tom isn't an accountant, and when the app asked if he uses the cash basis or the accrual basis of accounting he just picked one. "How different can they be?" he wondered.

Don't Go There Doug!

Doug gets paid pretty frequently in cash, and sometimes he isn't careful about depositing the cash in his business bank account. Sometimes he spends that cash on personal expenses, like snow cones, thinking, "How will anyone know?" Don't go there, Doug! Account for every cent of cash you earn in your business – you definitely don't want to get in trouble for underreporting income. If you think the IRS won't find out, you could be wrong, and if you underreport your income the IRS can go back and audit every return you have filed for your business. See "Common Tax Misconceptions" for some examples of how the IRS can be creative when catching people doing this kind of thing.

Well, they can be very different. Generally speaking, almost every small business will be a cash basis business (if you're not sure, it's highly likely your business is cash basis). If Tom's business was a cash basis business (and it was) but he selected "accrual" on his accounting app, the app will report revenue that he hasn't received yet, and that's obviously not a good thing. The app could also deduct bills that haven't been paid yet, and if the IRS finds those in an audit they could result in interest and penalties being applied.

This story is a great example of why it's good to find a tax professional who can work with you year-round. When questions come up, you can get an answer right away.

Questions for your tax professional:
1. Is my business cash basis or accrual basis?
2. What bookkeeping system do you recommend?
3. When is a deposit income versus a loan or capital contribution?

How Leonard deducts the most business miles possible

Tax savings potential: $$$$

Key topics in this story:
Tax
- Business mileage - how to track it.
- What vehicle expenses are deductible even if you use the standard mileage rate?

Business mileage is deductible. Pretty much everyone knows that, right? What people don't know is that there is a right way and a wrong way to log and deduct business miles to get the biggest deduction possible, and to document correctly to defend your mileage. One thing that many people don't know is that commuting is never deductible, but it's the way that "commuting" is defined that gives us some ideas. Commuting is simply traveling from your home to your first work location, and there is no rule that says your home can't be your first work location.

Leonard provides an excellent example. Leonard is an inventor and a tinkerer, and even though he has a full-time career, he also has a couple of patents that he's always building businesses around, or at least trying to get licensed. His is a classic "home run swing" business. He has an office in his home and he rents a P.O. box near his house in order to avoid putting his home address on business correspondence. Let's look at his business mileage on a normal Saturday, where he spends time in his home office and running errands related to his business. Leonard rolls out of bed and after breakfast and a shower he "commutes" down the hall to his home office, where he checks email, plans his day, and makes a call or two. Next he drives to the home improvement store to buy plumbing gaskets he's going to re-purpose as parts for a prototype he's working on. He runs some more errands and finally visits a computer store to pick up a new power cord before grabbing his mail at his P.O. box and then returning home.

Most people without a home office could not deduct the mileage from their home to the home improvement center, because travel from home to the first business location is never deductible. However, because Leonard's first business location is his home office, then the distance from the home office to the home improvement center is clearly mileage from the first business location to the second, and thus that mileage is deductible. The rest of Leonard's mileage as he runs his business errands is deductible, but mileage home is not. However, because Leonard's last errand is his P.O. box and the P.O. box is very close to home, he only misses out on the last mile or so from the post office to his house. Of course, if he needed to visit his home office before quitting for the day, then the last mile home would be deductible as well.

Records Check
If you use an app to track mileage, it's a good idea to save a backup every month or so. You never know when an app will no longer be supported, or maybe you "update" it only to find all of your data erased.

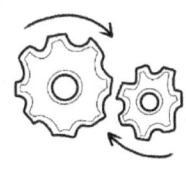

Leonard uses an app when he drives to track his mileage. He simply turns on the app, indicates that his miles are business miles, inputs a few other pieces of data, and the app tracks his mileage and populates a record of his business miles in real time.

Don't Go There Doug!
Doug drops his kids off at school every day on his way to work, and every day he pesters the crossing guard about becoming a client in his business. He figures that since he spoke to a potential client about business, then his mileage from his kid's school to his office is deductible. Don't go there, Doug! The personal element of taking his kids to school already makes this stop quite difficult to justify for business reasons, and simply asking the same person the same question every day does not make business sense.

Like many people, Leonard deducts the standard rate for his business miles, but what most people don't know is that he can also deduct the business portions of the interest on his vehicle loan and the taxes he pays to operate it. Parking fees are deductible in addition to mileage, and all it takes is writing down how much Leonard spent in order to claim the deduction. One other category that people often forget is tolls, and Leonard deducts those, too. Once upon a time a toll was two quarters tossed into a basket with no receipt. It was too little to worry about, too inconvenient to track, and too infrequent to add up to much. These days tolls are more expensive and more common, but most importantly, they're extremely easy to track. Leonard simply logs onto his mileage app that tells him when he was on business when he drove on a toll road, and then he checks his online toll tag account to grab the amounts he paid. The whole thing takes him about fifteen minutes at the end of the year, and it's a deduction of a couple of hundred dollars. That doesn't sound like much, but Leonard is in the 25% tax bracket, thus a deduction of $200 saves him $50. Spending 15 minutes to earn $50 means that Leonard was "paying" himself $200 per hour to research his toll expenses. When you look at it that way, even small tax deductions can be worthwhile!

Finally, occasionally Leonard's spouse needs to use a different car to run a business related errand. Leonard is sure to capture these miles and record them alongside his mileage, because any miles driven for business, regardless of whose car, or who's driving, are deductible. At over fifty cents per mile, this can add up fast!

> **Questions for your tax professional:**
> 1. What records do I need to maintain to justify my mileage deduction?
> 2. What is considered commuting if I have a home office?
> 3. What if I use more than one car for business?
> 4. What if my spouse drives his or her car for my business (like running an errand, bringing me something I forgot, etc)?

Michael A. York, EA
Andrew L. Stevens, EA, MBA

How a company got a big deduction for donating inventory

Tax savings potential: $$$

Key topics in this story:
Tax
- How to get a fat deduction for getting rid of old inventory.

Business
- How to build goodwill and brand equity with "distressed" inventory.

Recently a well-known musical instrument company (we'll call it "Goodstrings") found itself in hot water after a video surfaced of an excavator running over around 400 guitars, intentionally destroying them. At the time, Goodstrings was rebuilding its reputation following a very public bankruptcy and leadership overhaul. The company's future looked bright with a new CEO, a popular online "influencer" who was hired to oversee the company's brand experience, and a well-received mid-year product launch.

Then, things got a little worse when Goodstrings uploaded and subsequently pulled an online video that many people felt threatened other manufacturers while scolding the company's customer base. This video caused a controversial, years-old trademark infringement suit to garner a lot of attention online, and then the aforementioned video dropped that showed an excavator running over what looked like perfectly good guitars. For a lot of people, this was the worst blow to Goodstring's reputation yet.

Why would Goodstrings do such a thing? These were (by appearances) playable guitars. The guitars were completely assembled, with strings, tuners, and pickups, and yet they were intentionally destroyed. The short answer is that Goodstrings ran over the guitars because they wanted a big tax deduction, which we will explain shortly. We'll also tell you how they could have gotten the same tax deduction without damaging their goodwill with the guitar-playing community (their customer base).

Why would they destroy these guitars rather than donate them to a school or charity? To understand this question, we need to know some background information. Goodstrings released a guitar we'll call the Phoenix T in 2011 for a price of $4,000, and sales were disappointing. The guitar featured all of the things most people don't want in an electric guitar, and that no one wants in a heritage brand: Automatic tuners, a bunch of onboard effects, a USB jack to connect the guitar to your computer, and a really ugly paint scheme. Oh, and despite tons of features and even more knobs and switches, the guitar didn't ship with a manual. Weird.

The result is that Goodstrings was stuck about 400 unsellable Phoenix T guitars taking up space in a warehouse. It's understandable that the company would want to get rid of these guitars, and it's understandable that they would want to get some benefit from doing so. That leaves a few options: Selling the guitars, giving them away, or throwing them away. Let's look at each option.

If Goodstrings sold the guitars they might get a fraction of the original $4,000 price tag. For the sake of an example, let's say the company could sell each guitar for $1,000. Let's also assume that the company's basis in the guitars (basically what they spent to make each guitar, including raw materials, cost to manufacture and assemble, factory overhead, and more) is $1,500 per guitar. If they sold the guitars, they would take a $500 loss on each one, plus they would incur selling expenses. Let's not forget that their network of dealers wouldn't want to stock these particular instruments (who would want to take a perfectly good product off the wall in order to try to sell a Phoenix T?), and the brand would be tarnished at least a little from selling old, poorly-received guitars for a fraction of what a new Goodstrings usually commands. However, at least the $500 loss per guitar would be deductible, so the company would get that benefit.

If Goodstrings gave the guitars away to a charitable organization, they would get a tax deduction of the lesser of the Fair Market Value (FMV) or the basis. In our example above, the $1000 FMV is lower than the $1500 basis, so the company's tax deduction for donating the guitars would be $1000 per guitar. So at least in this example it is very likely that donating the guitars would be preferable to selling them.

Michael A. York, EA
Andrew L. Stevens, EA, MBA

> ### Don't go there Doug!
> Doug is in the business of selling refurbished computers, and occasionally some of his inventory is unsellable (or so he claims). He records a video of himself destroying one or two computers, and then claims that all of the computers were destroyed as distressed inventory. Next, Doug sells the remaining computers at deep discounts, and doesn't report the revenue. Don't go there, Doug! This amounts to tax fraud, and it's illegal. Anyone who asks us about something like this gets the same response: It's better to sleep well than to eat well. In other words, you might get away with it, but the stress of knowing you cheated isn't worth it (not to mention the penalties!). No qualified tax professional will work with clients who engage in such activities.

Finally, there's what Goodstrings did, which was to essentially throw the guitars away. The tax code specifies that unsellable (often called "distressed") inventory can be "written off" (deducted) for the basis of the inventory. In this example, that's $1500 per guitar. The IRS is pretty clear about how this needs to be done – they want proof that the inventory was distressed, and they want proof it was destroyed. They're the IRS after all – documentation is the name of their game, and they don't want someone to claim they destroyed the inventory and then sell it out the back door. That's why a video was made showing all of the guitars getting run over with an excavator: to document that the inventory was destroyed. Now, were the guitars really unsellable? Were they dangerous, as the company claimed? We'll never know, because the guitars were destroyed and trashed. In the end, Goodstrings was able to write off the full basis of each guitar ($1500 in our example).

Even though trashing the guitars provides the biggest tax deduction, it sure wasn't good for public relations. Is there a better strategy? Yes! Is there one that would potentially allow Goodstrings to get a full $1500 deduction for the guitars, while also benefiting charity (and the brand's goodwill)? Yes! How would such a strategy work? Let's talk about it!

As we discussed, Goodstrings might get $1000 for selling each of these guitars, but they have an issue in terms of their network of suppliers probably not wanting to stock (ahem) a turd. Luckily, there exists plenty of outlets for selling gear online, from Goodstrings's website to third party platforms. Goodstrings could have put together a press release stating that as part of their emergence from bankruptcy they would be liquidating some old gear through an online storefront. They could promote a contest or two, or maybe show some customers' unique uses for this heavily discounted gear. And most important of all, they could announce that every cent of the proceeds from these sales would go to a charitable organization, perhaps one that funds after school music programs across the country. They might get ribbed a little for selling old, less desirable instruments, but the goodwill earned from sponsoring music-centered charities would be worth it.

But what about the tax deduction? By destroying the guitars, Goodstrings got to write off the full basis of each guitar, which was $1500. We already showed that if Goodstrings sold the guitars, they would get to write off the difference between the basis of each guitar and the sales price. In our example that was a $500 write-off per guitar ($1500 in basis minus $1000 Fair Market Value). To write off the rest of the basis of each guitar, Goodstrings could simply donate the $1000 revenue from each guitar sold, allowing them to deduct an additional $1000 per guitar. That's a $1500 deduction per guitar – the same as if they ran over them with an excavator – while gaining a truckload of goodwill with their customer base and benefitting worthwhile charitable organizations.

We know that story will likely apply to very few people, though for those who can benefit, it presents a great strategy. The main reason we present this example is that it shows how there are plenty of options in the tax code to accomplish a desired result, and thus it makes sense to hire a competent tax professional and consult them before you do something that might have unintended consequences beyond your tax liability.

Michael A. York, EA
Andrew L. Stevens, EA, MBA

Hot Tax Tip
Don't trash inventory if you can help it. If possible, sell the inventory, deduct the write down and donate the proceeds of the sales. You get the same deduction as if you trashed the inventory, and you might get some positive goodwill out of it.

Questions for your tax professional:
1. What constitutes "distressed inventory" as it relates to my business?
2. Do I have distressed inventory, and if so, can I benefit from selling it and donating any proceeds?

Leigh and Cassy's Handmade Mugs: A bit of a capstone

Tax savings potential: $$$$$

Key topics in this story:
Tax
- Partnership expenses when each partner isn't in agreement.
- Hire your kids: how to deduct braces, cell phones, and private school.
- How to get your child a nice retirement or college savings account with tax-free money.
- How to borrow from retirement accounts to fund your business.
- Buying assets on credit: a big deduction now, smaller payments in the future.
- Contributing assets to a partnership: more of the Midas Touch!

Business
- SBA loans: how do they work?
- Do you really need to write a business plan?
- What are the key aspects of a business plan?
- Partner duties and compensation: what's fair?
- Planning for how the partnership will end: a big key to keeping your partnership from ending.
- Managing partner relations: often more work than managing the business.

Leigh and Cassy share a passion for pottery, and they met in a community pot-throwing space years ago. They got to know each other over time and admired each other's work. They had each been running their own small businesses specializing in handmade ceramic items, and they had each mainly sold their wares online and at art fairs.

Leigh's son worked for a well-known coffee company that did a lot of philanthropic work with veterans' groups. The problem was, the coffee company sold a selection of mugs along with their coffee, but all of the mugs were made in China, which the company decided didn't fit with their all-American brand. They needed to add an American-made mug to their product line. One day when Leigh and Cassy were together at the kiln working on their pottery, Leigh told Cassy all about the issue with the Chinese-made mugs. Cassy has a background in business, and she had an idea: The two of them could partner together to lease space to produce mugs, and then hire some workers to do the bulk of the work. With Leigh's connection to the coffee company they could offer to create a custom mug with logos and branding and a handmade touch that a mass-producer couldn't duplicate. And of course, these mugs would be made in America.

After speaking with an attorney, Leigh and Cassy decided to form a partnership for their new venture. They are equal partners, with each owning 50% of the company, and they agreed early on to split time, money, and effort equally.

Cassy and Leigh each owning their own pottery businesses and partnering in a second one presented some unique challenges for their businesses, but also some opportunities. Some expenses are very obviously expenses of the partnership, such as their employees who work for the partnership and the supplies and equipment used to make the specialty mugs. Rent for their kiln space is obviously also a partnership-level expense. But what if one of the partners wanted to use the kiln or throwing stations when they're not in use making mugs? Or what if one of them wanted to expense a pottery class that the other didn't think made sense for the partnership's business needs? These kinds of issues are very common in partnerships, and they can be very difficult to resolve when each partner owns 50% of the company.

Remember how each of the partners also owned her own pottery business? It turns out this is what enabled the partners to avoid some of the challenges mentioned above. For example, if one of the partners wanted to attend a pottery class and the other didn't, then the partner who attended can simply use that expense in her own wholly-owned pottery business and not expense it to the partnership. Naturally, the business that took on the expense would also get 100% of the benefit of the tax deduction. Deciding what expenses are reasonable and necessary for any partnership to pay for can be very tricky and is one of the main sources of strife between partners. We will discuss other "tricky" situations like profit distributions, "equal" efforts, and "equal" time later, but keep this idea in mind, as this is one way that partners can avoid these kinds of issues.

When we talk with our clients, we often bring up the idea of finding deductions among existing expenses because it's a powerful one. If you think about it, it just makes sense: when looking for tax deductions, start with expenses you were going to incur anyway. In other words, if you had to choose between these two options, which would you choose: Option A, which is a $5000 overhaul of a machine that is due in four years, or Option B, which is $5000 for your kid's braces that she needs right now? You might say, "Wait, one of those is clearly a business expense, and the other isn't." You're right. But still, if you could deduct the braces and put off the overhaul until it's due, wouldn't you do that? Ok, now let's work backwards and figure out how to deduct the braces.

The answer is actually very simple: You can't deduct the braces as a business expense, but you can hire your kid and let her pay for her own braces. This leads us to an interesting topic of discussion that is probably beyond the scope of this book, but everyone's first reaction to this idea is: "My kids don't want to work for me." Curiously, when we ask people how they developed their strong character and sound work ethic, they tell us about how their parents used to make them get up early and go to work on the family farm or in the family business. This isn't a parenting book, but consider for a second that you might actually be doing your kids a favor by having them work in your business (even if they don't see it that way now).

Here is an example of how Cassy did it: Cassy's daughter was 14 years old, and she attended private school. On certain days she would join her mom to work at the business, doing light cleaning and office administrative tasks. A lot of people have their kids do chores around the house for an allowance, but Cassy simply swapped it and hired her daughter to do light work around her business. Her daughter's total compensation for the year came out to about $6000.00.

> <u>Hot Tax Tip</u>
> Hiring your kids to do work at your business is a great way to get a tax deduction for money you were going to spend on them anyway.

Michael A. York, EA
Andrew L. Stevens, EA, MBA

Cassy drafted an employment agreement for her daughter. Next, she set up a bank account for her daughter, and all of her daughter's wages were deposited into the bank account directly from the business account. Because the daughter was under age 17 and the entity wasn't structured as a corporation, FICA withholding wasn't necessary. Also, because the amount of the wages was below the standard deduction amount, there were no state or federal taxes, either. In other words, the wages paid to the daughter were totally untaxed, but the business could claim a deduction for the amount she was paid. Cassy usually paid for her daughter's private school education, but it's totally legal for her daughter to chip in, too. And that's what they did. The $6,000 she earned wasn't enough to totally cover the cost of tuition, but every little bit helps, and in a roundabout way the business took a tax deduction for paying for part of Cassy's daughter's private school.

Records Check
When hiring a family member be sure to deposit funds directly from the business account to the family member's account.

Other options for that $6,000 were to fund a Roth IRA or a 529 college savings account, which each allow for tax free retirement or college funds. Think about that: saving for college or retirement with money that was never taxed, and (unless the laws change) will never be taxed. That is the way to stretch your investment dollar!

> ### *Don't Go There Doug!*
> Doug hired his toddler twins to work in his business doing light office duties. He pays them $55 per hour, and they work a few hours every day when they're home from daycare. Don't go there, Doug! What can a toddler do in an office that would command $55 per hour? The only thing we can think of is paying the kids $55 for every hour they don't break something, and that's not a real job. If your kids aren't doing real work that they're capable of doing and at a reasonable wage, this strategy isn't going to work.

Some technical notes (skip this if you already have your tax pro on the phone to discuss this strategy): One of the keys to this strategy is how the business is structured in terms of its choice of entity. If it's a sole proprietorship, single member LLC (more or less the same thing as a sole proprietorship for tax purposes), a partnership where each of the partners is a parent of the employed child (in other words, if there are two partners they need to each be a parent to the child), or an LLC where the members are each parents of the child, then no withholding is necessary. If the business is a corporation, or a partnership where not every partner is a parent of the employed child, then withholding is necessary. In Cassy's case, if her partnership with Leigh hired Cassy's daughter, they would have to withhold FICA from the daughter's paycheck. However, we already discussed that Cassy had her own business outside of the partnership. Cassy and Leigh simply contracted with Cassy's business to perform certain duties, and Cassy's business hired her daughter to do the work.

When it came time to finance their new venture Cassy and Leigh had to decide among some options. They could simply use their own savings to purchase the kiln and other equipment and to lease their space. They could take out a Small Business Administration (SBA) loan. They also considered borrowing from their retirement accounts. They decided against using savings because of the tax benefits of leverage (also called debt). Interest on debt payments is tax deductible, and by using debt financing they would still have savings to dip into if they needed quick cash. That left an SBA loan and borrowing from their retirement accounts. Let's talk about the last one next.

Most employer retirement accounts like 401(k)s will not let you borrow against your account. What does that even mean? Borrowing from a retirement account (or borrowing against: same thing) means you take money out of the account, but you have to pay it back, plus interest. If the money isn't paid back per the terms of the loan some steep tax penalties can accrue. Likewise, Individual Retirement Accounts (IRAs) and Roth IRAs also do not allow you to borrow against them. However, retirement accounts can very easily be rolled over from one type of account to another. If you've ever left a job where you had a retirement account through your employer, you probably rolled it over from the account with your employer to an IRA or possibly to your new employer's account. Here's where we figure out how to borrow against these accounts: Cassy and Leigh, as owners of their new partnership, could set up a retirement account sponsored by the partnership. When they create this new retirement plan, they can write-in a section that allows participants to borrow funds. Then, all they have to do is roll their 401(k)s and IRAs into their own accounts at the new retirement account sponsored by the partnership - the one that allows for borrowing. In case you're wondering, no, their money wouldn't be co-mingled, and it also wouldn't become the partnership's money. They could also roll their accounts back into an IRA or other retirement account whenever it was convenient for them.

> *Hot Tax Tip*
> Owning a business often means you can create a retirement plan that fits your needs, and it may allow for more savings than a regular 401(k)!

Why borrow against their own retirement accounts? Whether the partnership borrowed from a bank or borrowed from the partners' retirement accounts, the partnership has to pay interest. If the partnership borrows from the partners' retirement accounts, the business is paying interest back to the retirement account rather than to the bank. Since interest is tax deductible, the partnership would get a tax deduction for the interest, and the interest and principle would be paid into the retirement account. There are very good reasons not to borrow against a retirement account, the main ones being risk and opportunity cost. The risk is that if the business can't pay back the loan it means your retirement account takes a big hit, and there will be penalties charged by the IRS, as well. The opportunity cost is that you lose the opportunity to earn higher returns in the stock market. In other words, if you take money out of your retirement account that is invested in a few stocks earning 20% returns (for example), and you are only paying 5% interest to your account, then you are choosing to earn 5% interest instead of having the opportunity to earn 20% from the stocks you were invested in. Still, under the right circumstances, borrowing from a retirement account can be a good option.

That brings us to SBA loans. SBA stands for Small Business Administration (part of the federal government), and as the name implies, these loans are designed specifically for small businesses. There are many types of loans available, but we will just cover the basics. These are loans made by local lenders (banks, credit unions, etc.). The loans are guaranteed by the SBA (government), and the terms can be quite flexible with low interest rates. The downside is that these loans can be difficult to get, and it can take some time to go through the process to get one. In other words, with an SBA loan, the money comes from your local bank, but the government takes on most of the risk of default, and thus the bank provides very attractive interest rates and repayment terms. These loans can be a great option if you qualify and if you can wait to go through the process. In the end, Cassy and Leigh decided an SBA loan was best for their business.

One of the first major purchases for the partnership was a kiln, which they purchased on credit rather than paying for it up front using the funds from their SBA loan. Even though they make payments on the kiln, it's still a purchase, and the tax laws are different than if they were making similar rent payments. When renting a piece of equipment, you can take a tax deduction for just the amount of the rent you pay per year. Simple. When you purchase a piece of equipment, you get to deduct either full amount of the purchase, or you can choose to depreciate the equipment over a few years regardless of whether you purchase it on credit or pay for the whole thing up front (this gets complicated: talk to your tax professional!). Of course, if you finance the purchase the interest payments are tax deductible as well. In Cassy and

Leigh's case, they could take a big deduction for the full amount of the cost of the kiln even though they were making payments, which added up to a big tax savings.

> *Hot Tax Tip*
> You get the full tax benefit of a purchase right away even if you finance it and actually pay for it over a period of years.

In their second-year, sales were very strong and they were looking for tax deductions around December, just before the new year started and the financials from the current year became locked. The keys to smart tax deductions are twofold: 1) It's often smarter to deduct as much as you can, as soon as you can. To put it another way, a bird in the hand is worth two in the bush and getting a tax deduction now might be better if there is a chance the laws will change (leading to the deduction to disappear in the future). There is also a "time value of money," which means that a dollar you save now is worth more than a dollar you save in the future, because the dollar you save now can be invested, and due to the magic of compound interest, will grow over time. 2) Tax deductions should come from money you were going to spend anyway. Believe it or not, a lot of people look for tax deductions in places where they weren't planning to spend money, and that is ultimately a waste and not a great business move. The trick is to look for places you were going to spend money anyway and strategize to turn those into deductions.

> *Records Check*
> A written business plan and financial model is a great place to look for opportunities to invest in your own business.

When the partnership was formed each of the partners contributed assets to it, which is very common. In almost every partnership, the partners bring cash and other more tangible assets with them, and after the contribution, the business controls those assets. The cash goes into the business bank account, and the tangible assets (tools, equipment, and so on) get written down in ledger showing which partner contributed them, and the fair market value of each thing. The business gets to depreciate those assets over several years and the business gets to deduct that depreciation against its income.

> ### Hot Tax Tip
> Contributing assets to a partnership is similar to converting assets from personal use to business use. You have the Midas Touch!

Cassy and Leigh took their idea to Leigh's son, and he took it to his bosses, who said, "Can we see a business plan?" Being still in the idea phase, Cassy and Leigh hadn't written one yet. There are a lot of great books out there on how to write a business plan, and so we're not going to go deep on that subject, but we will emphasize a few things that Cassy and Leigh learned, and some key areas they focused on. First, it's very common for new businesses to need a business plan to show investors and potential customers. Investors and clients like to see that sufficient careful thought has been put into the concept of the business. The plan is a window into the way the founders think, and it can be very revealing. The business plan is also a signal that the founders are serious about the business: these plans can take a lot of time and effort to write, and the level of detail required of a good business plan can show the passion of the founders in a way that a sales pitch over the phone cannot.

Cassy and Leigh spent extra time on a few key messages that are important to investors and clients, and those are management, market, and momentum. You might be wondering why potential customers would be so concerned about these things, and the reason is that the coffee company had several proposals from different companies who wanted to supply mugs, and it was important to them to choose the best supplier. Agreeing to work with a supplier that wasn't well-managed and didn't understand its own market could result in a poor supply of product, and that would cost the client time and money. In any case, Cassy and Leigh made sure to convey their expertise with ceramics and pottery, and they provide great detail into how they would produce the mugs, the quantity they could supply, and things like lead times for new orders. They also put a lot of thought into the potential market the coffee company could reach with these mugs and gave some prospective sales and profit figures. Finally, they forecast where the market could go (the momentum) based on cultural trends and other factors.

While writing the plan Cassy and Leigh learned a ton about their business. When they put together the numbers for their financials, they realized that they couldn't afford to buy raw materials from a certain supplier, and they had to negotiate some discounts from a few other suppliers. They also learned that they each thought they would be doing certain tasks, and there was quite a bit of overlap they had to discuss. As you can imagine, there were other tasks that neither of them wanted to do, and they had to figure out who would perform those roles, or whether they could hire someone to perform them and how that person's wages fit into their budget.

> ### Business Tip
> You should think of a business plan sort of like a soft-opening for your business. You get to learn a lot and make mistakes that don't cost anything, and you take those lessons with you when you have your grand opening.

A very common belief among people new to partnerships is that each partner will perform equal efforts to the other partners, and thus it will be totally fair when each partner is compensated equally. In reality, that **never** happens. Discussing partnership compensation can be a very uncomfortable topic, but it's much more uncomfortable (downright nasty) to discuss it later on, when one partner feels he or she has done all the work, and the other partner still wants an equal share of the proceeds. Rather than plan for equal efforts, Cassy and Leigh put a lot of thought into each task that would need to be done in order to run the business. There was shipping, packaging, payroll, supervising employees, scheduling shifts, banking, record keeping, marketing, managing the website and social media, and many other things. They did their best to estimate how much time and effort each of those things would require, and they divided them up as equally as they could. They also agreed to come back to the table in a month after doing all of these tasks to see if they had indeed divided them up fairly. This way, there would hopefully be less conflict later on about who was doing more work, and thus how cash proceeds should be paid out.

Another common thing that new partners almost never consider is how the business will be terminated. It's called "planning the divorce before the wedding," and pretty much no one does it. Imagine going into business with a new partner, and over time it becomes clear that the business isn't going to work. At what point do you throw in the towel? At what point do you both write checks from your personal savings to keep the business afloat? What about the assets you each contributed at the beginning? What about any outstanding debts that need to be paid for? What if a space your business is renting needs to be cleaned out, or assets sold off, or inventory liquidated? All of these things should be discussed and agreed to – in writing – by the partners ahead of time, otherwise they become major problems when a partnership relationship is strained by an unsuccessful business.

> <u>Business Tip</u>
> If you're uncomfortable discussing these issues with your partner before you go into business, you're going into business with the wrong partner.

Even if the business is doing well there can be "divorce" issues that can come into play. What if the business is going great, but one partner wants out? Can they simply sell to any old random Joe, or does the existing partner have a say? Or worse, what if the business is doing well and one partner stops contributing, but still wants a payout? Can the other partner buy them out, and if so, under what terms? Speaking to an attorney about all of these issues and getting them resolved in writing before commencing with the business is one of the best pieces of advice we can give, and Cassy and Leigh did just that.

There is an old saying in business: "What is the one ship that won't sail? A partnership." For all of the reasons we just discussed, managing partnership relations can take more work than running the business itself. If you are going to start a partnership, the most important thing to work on is communication. Otherwise: mistakes happen, feelings get hurt, trust is damaged, and ultimately the business suffers. Decide to communicate and make it as important as anything in the business plan. Make sure phone calls get answered promptly, and that emails and texts get returned as soon as possible. Log and store decisions as if they were any other critical record the company will need in the future. Don't count on partners to remember conversations as well as you do.

> ### Business Tip
> Don't just tell your attorney how to draw up the partnership agreement. Get him or her to give you real advice about how to structure your partnership agreement and follow that advice

Cassy and Leigh are relentless about communication, and it has saved their relationship more than once. Here is a great example: They took a business trip to check out a much bigger operation in a different city so they could learn what it would take for them to expand their business, and when they got home Leigh placed an order for some upgraded equipment they had agreed to buy. When Cassy saw the bill, she was confused: this was more than they had agreed to spend, and it would mean they would be earning a smaller payout for the next six months.

However, when Cassy and Leigh had discussed the purchase over dinner, Cassy had taken notes, and at the end they had reviewed the notes and Leigh took a picture of the note page and emailed it to herself. When Cassy approached her about the purchase, Leigh simply retrieved the image of the notes and reviewed it. It turned out they had agreed to purchase the equipment, but only if it could be found in a certain price range. Leigh had forgotten about the price range part, but it was right there in the notes, and she cancelled the order until they could find something they could afford. This kind of thing is so common in partnerships, and it very often leads to big conflicts. The only solution is to be diligent about communicating constantly, and to maintain records of that communication. Disagreements lead to distrust, and that kills businesses.

> **Records Check**
> Save every email between you and your partners. If you have a phone call, take notes and email them to your partners after the call. If you have a business meeting, take a picture of your notes and save it. Never assume that everyone is on the same page, or that everyone will remember things the same way!

To recap, Cassy and Leigh met in an activity they shared, and after getting to know each other, they decided to go into business. Here are the key lessons to be learned from their story:

Each partner maintained their own "side" business so they could take advantage of opportunities that the other partner passed on, such as taking a deduction for certain classes.

They also considered borrowing against their retirement accounts to finance purchases for the business, which typically isn't possible unless you own a business and use it to sponsor a retirement plan with specific attributes.

Cassy employed her daughter to help in the business, and while the business got a nice deduction for the daughter's wages, Cassy's daughter didn't have to pay any tax on what she was paid.

Finally, Cassy and Leigh were careful to plan the divorce before the wedding, to overcommunicate, and to keep careful records of conversations and decisions. All this was in order to keep their partnership running smoothly, and so they could each spend more of their energy focusing on making money, and not on the headaches that come from having a partnership.

> **Questions for your tax professional:**
> 1. How can I take a tax deduction for paying my kids to work in my business?
> 2. How can I use my retirement savings to fund my business?
> 3. How can I structure my partnership to deduct expenses not agreed on by the other partner?
> 4. How can I contribute and distribute assets from my partnership?

Beth, and the one function you should always outsource

Tax savings potential: $$

Key topics in this story:
Business
- HR issues and how to deal with them.
- What can an HR outsourcer do for your business?

Beth operated a daycare and had fifteen full-time employees. She loved being around kids, especially the babies. She could change diapers all day long and rub tummies and wipe away tears and clean runny noses and never get tired of any of it. She loved the kids in her care, and thus their parents loved Beth. She created an amazing culture at her daycare center, and business was good.

As we said before, if you have a small business you need all the functions of a big business. Beth's business was no different: She needed a marketing department, a finance department, a treasury department, a human resources department, an operations department, etc. The only difference between a big business and Beth's business is that all of those functions are done by fewer people, and in Beth's case, they were all done by Beth. Since Beth had limited hours in the day, she needed to be judicious about where she spent her time, and thus she prioritized some of those tasks over others. Like most people in business, Beth spent her time on the things that made her money, and the things she enjoyed most about running a daycare center. In other words, she focused like a laser on marketing her services, she watched her receivables and payables diligently, and she was a hawk when it came to operating efficiently. She also carved out plenty of time during the day to be around the kids.

After a long day, how much time would you guess she spent reading up on employment law? How excited do you think she was to prepare quarterly payroll taxes? Did it make her money when one of her employees asked how much paid time off they had accrued, or if Beth could help them find last year's October pay stub? Like anyone with employees, Beth knew that her employees helped her make money, but dealing with HR issues did not.

One of the greatest feelings Beth received from running her business came from creating jobs that helped families put food on the table, and that feeling intensified when she was able to give her employees benefits, such as a company retirement plan. When Beth was finally able to put a retirement plan in place she was at a total loss as to where to begin. She couldn't name the types of employer-sponsored retirement plans, let alone know which one to choose or how to administer it. Moreover, spending her time on those things didn't help her business make money, and it surely didn't give her more time to spend with the children in her care.

And then the stakes were raised. An employee who had been trouble since day one, and whom Beth had recently fired, decided to sue her. Beth began to look into her predicament, and she found that the average out of court settlement for similar suits is about $40k, and if it went to litigation her total cost could be much, much higher. Beth had never planned for such a thing, and it put her business, and by extension, the well-being of "her" kids and her employees in jeopardy.

Beth was lucky, and the lawsuit didn't put her out of business. It did, however, make her rethink her priorities when it came to all of the business functions she kept in-house. She didn't want to outsource her marketing function: she liked marketing and she felt that no one could "sell" her business as well as she could. Likewise, she wasn't ready to turn over the reins of operating her daycare on a day-to-day basis. But at this point, outsourcing her HR function was a no-brainer. Everything to do with HR seemed like a massive liability, with zero potential for profit.

> ### Don't Go There Doug!
> Doug conducts his own hiring and doesn't use a third party to help him with HR functions. It's pretty common for him to ask candidates inappropriate questions like their age, their pregnancy status (now, or in the future), and he likes to talk about his personal relationships. A lot. Don't go there, Doug! Even if Doug got away with these actions for years, all it takes is one person to expose Doug's nonsense and sue the business out of existence. Doug would have no one to blame but himself.

Beth spoke to her tax professional, who recommended she retain a professional human resources firm that specializes in small businesses. She learned that the right firm can help her with payroll and automated clocking-in/out, as well as her quarterly payroll taxes and annual reports. She can even opt for an HR function that helps with onboarding, firing, applicant screening, and compliance with local and federal laws. The firm she hired even set up and administered the company retirement plan. She figured that all of this outsourcing would cost a fortune, but the quote she received was actually very reasonable. In some ways, she considered the cost something of an insurance policy against the prospect of another lawsuit, even if it's unlikely to happen again.

Most importantly, on a day to day basis, she doesn't have to help employees find an old pay stub or calculate their remaining PTO, because all of that is done for her. She also doesn't have to budget time to prepare quarterly payroll taxes (usually done late in the evening on the night before the due date), and she doesn't have to hunt down addresses to figure out where to send W2s every January. All of the time she saved by outsourcing her business's HR function is time she can spend on her business, or just changing a few diapers and rubbing a few tummies.

Questions for your tax professional:
1. What retirement accounts are appropriate for my business?
2. Can you recommend an HR / Payroll company?

Michael A. York, EA
Andrew L. Stevens, EA, MBA

Section Four – What if I'm a W2 employee (and I don't want to do any of this stuff)?

Not everyone wants to set up a business, despite the tremendous personal income and tax savings that can come from doing so. We get it. There is a "hassle factor" with all of this stuff, and maybe you're just not motivated by money (or maybe you are, but other priorities take precedence). Maybe your priority is your children, and time spent working on a business is time away from them, and you are the kind of parent who would *pay* to spend time with your kids. Whatever your reasons, how about some sound advice even if you don't want to start a business?

How Becky donates stocks (and avoids a lot of taxes)

Tax savings potential: $$$$

Key topics in this story:
Tax
- How to get a bigger deduction for your charitable contributions.
- How to donate stocks and pay less in capital gains tax later.

At a recent tax planning meeting, our client Becky told us how she was planning to make a sizable donation to her favorite charity. We've known Becky for a long time, and she has always been successful and generous (two of our favorite things). She was excited about helping out this organization, and she was proud she was in a position to do so. We're pretty familiar with Becky's finances (it's sort of our job), so we said, "Hey, let's think about this for a second: would you be interested in getting an even bigger tax savings?" Becky was interested.

Let's walk through how this donation works in most instances. Say Becky is donating $10k, and she's in the 35% regular tax bracket, and the 15% long term capital gains tax bracket. If Becky writes a check from her personal account for $10,000, she reduces her tax burden by $3,500, which is great. The math is very simple: it's $10k multiplied by her top tax rate, or 35%.

However, knowing Becky's finances, we know she has an extensive stock portfolio. We said, "Why not donate stock instead of cash?" Becky was intrigued. Let's say Becky has stock worth $10k, and her basis in the stock is $2k. That means if Becky wants to sell this particular stock, she would end up paying $1,600 in capital gains tax on the $8k gain ($10k sale price minus $2k basis).

> ### Hot Tax Tip
> Donating capital gain property means you get a full deduction for the fair market value of the item, and you get to avoid tax on any capital gains. The charity doesn't pay tax on the gain, either.

Well, if Becky donates the stock instead, she *never* pays capital gains tax for that stock, and she still gets the full tax deduction for the $10k fair market value. That means she still receives the $3,500 tax break as if she donated $10k in cash, but she also gets an additional $1,600 in the form of capital gains tax that she will avoid forever. The only real key here is that Becky has to donate stock that she has owned for over one year. That's it.

> ### Don't Go There Doug!
> Doug wants to sell his penny stock shares at a loss in order to get a tax deduction, and then he plans to repurchase the same shares right away. Don't go there, Doug! That's called a "wash sale" and the rules say we have to ignore that loss for tax purposes.

By donating stock instead of cash Becky got the same tax savings of $3,500, but she was also able to avoid capital gains tax on stock held in her portfolio - an additional tax savings of $1,600. Best of all, if she wishes she can replace the stock immediately without any taxes or penalties, and her basis in the new stock will be $10k.

Questions for your tax professional:
1. Can I donate stock and get a tax deduction, if so, how?
2. What is my long term capital gains rate?

Retirement Plans: Save now or pay later
Tax savings potential: $$$$$

Key topics in this story:
Tax
- The best tax deduction - saving taxes by paying your future self.
- How 401(k) employer matching works (free money!).

Save for your retirement. Seriously. We have a couple of stories to try to encourage you (and scare the crap out of you) to put money away for when you can no longer work.

First, let us tell you about Bob and Sarah. Bob and Sarah were wage-earners who never made more than $20 per hour. They lived modestly and raised three great kids, despite not having the financial resources that come with having high-flying careers. Their employers offered 401(k) plans, each with a matching provision. Bob and Sarah contributed as much as they could afford, but in lean times they sacrificed in order to contribute at least as much as they needed to in order to max out their employer's matching provision.

> *Hot Tax Tip*
> Max out 401(k) contributions at least to the point where you get matching from your employer. It's free money, and believe us, when you get to retirement age you will be glad you took advantage.

Let's explain 401(k) matching quickly. Most plans work like this: If your company offers a 401(k), the company will "match" a percentage of every dollar you contribute, up to a percentage of your yearly pay. Let's use an example where your company will "match" fifty cents on the dollar up to 6% of your pay, and say your annual pay is $40k. Here's how the math works out:

Pay:	$40,000	
6% of pay:	$2,400	(This is the max the company will contribute)
6% of pay @ $0.50:	$4,800	(This is the minimum you have to put in to make your company max-out its match)

Thus, if you wanted to take full advantage of your 401(k) matching, you would put $4,800 into your 401(k) per year, and the company would put in $2,400 on your behalf. That's $2,400 of free money that your company wouldn't have given you otherwise. It's almost like getting a raise for being smart about saving for retirement.

To take this example to its logical conclusion, we should also look at how much the $4,800 contribution costs after taxes. The contribution is made before tax, and in the example we're working with, the couple makes $40k per year, which puts them in the 12% federal bracket for 2019. If we assume they live in a state with income taxes, which average about 6%, that means the total combined income tax rate is 18% for this couple. 18% of $4,800 is $864, so by saving the $4,800 for retirement the couple saved $864 in tax. Thus, the

Michael A. York, EA
Andrew L. Stevens, EA, MBA

$4,800 actually only cost them $3,936, because if they had taken the cash instead of contributing to their retirement account they would have only received $3,936 after taxes. That's a $3,936 cash outlay for a retirement contribution of $7,200! Not bad at all! Let's take this one step further – after 20 years invested at 8%, an investment of $3,936 grows to $18,499, which is nothing to shake your head at. But when we add in the tax benefits of retirement savings and the free money from your employer, it grows to $33,559, and of course it's even better if you repeat the investment every year!

Back to Bob and Sarah: At about the age of 65 they decided to retire, and they were thrilled to see that their retirement savings had grown to two million dollars. With their retirement savings they were able to take amazing family trips (and bring the grandkids), buy a small cabin near a lake on a beautiful piece of property, and generally enjoy their lives. They honestly never thought they would end up this comfortable. They often said that they never missed the money they saved for retirement, because they never saw it: it just came out of their checks. But having that money grow and being able to retire with a big nest egg felt like winning the lottery at the exact moment they retired.

> ### *Don't go there Doug!*
> Doug has a retirement plan available through work, but he doesn't trust it, and he chooses not to use it. Even worse, Doug's "investment advisor" (who is really his eccentric uncle), who doesn't understand Doug's full financial profile, tells him to simply invest his retirement funds in an IRA (so that he can control the investments). The problem is, Doug makes too much money to qualify for a deductible IRA, and he doesn't do the proper record keeping to track his non-deductible contributions (because his uncle didn't tell him to). Don't go there, Doug! Retirement plans have lots of rules, and we suggest you only take retirement planning advice from a trusted advisor who understands your full financial profile.

Now, to scare the crap out of you. Nick was a lawyer, and his wife stayed at home taking care of their three children. Nick made amazing money, and his family never felt the sting of tight finances the way Bob and Sarah's family had. They lived in a million-dollar house, they took lavish European trips every summer and went skiing every winter, and they had any material possession they wanted. Here's the rub: no one in the family ever saved any money. Nick completely ignored his retirement savings, despite having retirement plans he could have adopted in his law practice. His wife also never contributed to an IRA, despite our recommendations that she do so. Nick planned to continue to practice law (which he loved to do) until age 70, and he planned to start socking away cash from age 60 to 70 to fund his retirement. Between the cash he would save and the proceeds from downsizing their home, Nick and his wife counted on having a comfortable retirement.

We bet at this point you think Nick died. He didn't. If he had, it might have been better for his family's finances (if we're allowed to say that). At age 58, Nick had a stroke that left him debilitated and unable to practice law. His family had no significant savings, and Nick's plans to fund his retirement were shot. His medical expenses ate up a good part of the proceeds from downsizing the house, and the money he received from a disability insurance policy and Social Security were barely enough to pay the remaining bills. Unlike Bob and Sarah, Nick's story ends with his wife and him spending their golden years working hourly wage jobs.

Man, that story is a bummer. Save for retirement, and take advantage of that free 401(k) money! And if your company doesn't offer a 401(k), talk to your tax professional or financial advisor about how you can save for retirement.

Questions for your tax professional:
1. How much do I need to contribute to my 401(k) to at least max out the matching provision?
2. At my tax bracket, how much do I save for every dollar contributed to retirement?
3. What other retirement plans are available in addition to my 401(k)?
4. Can you help me roll over my old 401(k)'s into my IRAs?

Glenn gets to deduct charitable contributions without itemizing

Tax savings potential: $$$

Key topics in this story:
Tax
- How to lower your required minimum distribution and avoid tax.
- How to deduct charitable contributions without itemizing.

Every time someone campaigned on the promise to simplify the tax code, our mentor Gary would say that their real goal was to take away deductions from American taxpayers. Well, the Tax Cuts and Jobs Act is here, and with it came the deletion and reduction of many common deductions on the Schedule A (the form that allows people to deduct things like mortgage interest, state taxes, charitable contributions, etc.) To offset the changes in the Schedule A there were some other provisions added to help folks save taxes, but in our opinion, Gary may have had a point about this one.

Let's take a look at some of the changes. For starters, State and Local Taxes (SALT) are capped at $10,000. Interest on home equity loans is no longer deductible except for specific circumstances, like using the funds to make a business purchase (talk to your tax pro). Casualty and theft loss deductions are gone unless the loss happened in a Federally-declared disaster area. Finally, miscellaneous expenses – including employee business expenses, job hunting expenses, investment fees, and tax preparation fees (that one hurts...) – a are no longer deductible for most people. That means millions of Americans who used to be able to take a deduction for job-related expenses like mileage, travel, and meals, are now out of luck.

So, the Schedule A has been altered, and at the same time the standard deduction amount went way up. The net result is that many taxpayers who used to itemize deductions will now be claiming the standard deduction. One bright side is that retired people can benefit from these changes. "How?" you say, especially considering that many retired people have substantial charitable contributions, and they will no longer get a tax benefit from making those donations? Let's take a closer look.

> *Hot Tax Tip*
> If you are required to make "RMDs" (required minimum distributions), or will be soon, get in touch with your IRA trustee immediately if you plan to make even a single cent of charitable contributions for the year.

Our friend Glenn doesn't itemize (he and his wife take the standard deduction), but he still gets to "write off" his charitable contributions. Glenn and his wife have to make required minimum distributions from their IRAs every year, and they have to pay tax on that money. The key is that Glenn knows a trick for how to give some of that money to charity before it ever gets to him. It's called a "Qualified Charitable Distribution."

Here's how it works: Glenn instructs the trustee of his IRA (his wife does the same out of her own IRA account) to write a check directly to his charity of choice (Glenn and his wife don't touch the money – this is important). In their case, it's their local church. The trustee writes the check to the church, reduces the required minimum distribution (or RMD: more on these later) by the amount of the donation, and then pays out the remaining RMD to Glenn. When Glenn receives his 1099-R, the amount Glenn directed the trustee to give to the church is not listed as taxable income, and Glenn obviously isn't taxed on it.

> **Don't Go There Doug!**
> Doug gave cash to his favorite in-law (who has always been a bit of a charity case), who wanted new Baja lights for his Gremlin. Then he found out about qualified charitable distributions, after he had taken his RMDs in cash. He claimed on his tax return that his gift to his in-law was a qualified charitable distribution, when it was not. Don't go there, Doug! It's very easy for the IRS to check on this stuff. Do it the right way, or not at all!

If Glenn took the full RMD and then wrote a check to his church out of his personal checking account he would get zero tax benefit for the donation, *and* his RMD would be higher by the amount of his donation, meaning he would be taxed on it. In Glenn's case, because he directs his IRA trustee to make the payment from his Required Minimum Distribution, he still gets to take a deduction, even without a Schedule A.

Another thing we love about this strategy is how it lowers something called "adjusted gross income" (AGI), which is also called "above the line income." There's no wonder why everyone finds taxes so confusing – not only are there major changes every few years, there are multiple confusing terms for everything! In a nutshell, what we're talking about is income on the first page of your tax return. If we can lower that number, it tends to have follow-on effects on other aspects of the tax return, and they're pretty much all positive. In Glenn's case, making his charitable contributions out of his RMDs means he also pays less tax on his social security benefits, so it's like getting two deductions for the price of one! For more information on how lowering AGI tends to result in paying less tax on social security, check out Janet and Kyle's story.

> **Questions for your tax professional:**
> 1. When do I need to start taking required minimum distributions?
> 2. How much is my RMD, and how much will I be taxed on it?
> 3. Will I get additional benefits from lowering my adjusted gross income by using a qualified charitable distribution?

Here's a great tip about Roth IRAs
Tax savings potential: $$

Key topics in this story:
Tax
- Straight dope on Roth IRAs.
- Get your Roth IRA 5-year clock started immediately.

A Roth IRA is a common retirement plan that allows you to contribute to $6,000 per year after tax, meaning, you don't get a tax deduction for money you put in. The money grows tax free until you retire, and any money you withdraw once you retire is tax free. That "tax free" part sounds great, but forgive us if we're skeptical. Once upon a time social security benefits weren't taxed, but that changed, and we believe that at some point in the future our cash-strapped government might find a way to tax Roth IRA earnings. In other words, if you ever get a choice between getting a tax deduction now or a tax deduction in 20 years, it's tough to argue against taking the deduction now.

When would you prefer to take a deduction: when you're in your prime earning years, or when you are in retirement? You are likely to be in a higher tax bracket when are in your prime earning years, and thus you get a bigger tax benefit for taking a deduction against a higher tax rate. If you are in a higher tax bracket now than when you retire, then you should contribute to your traditional IRA instead of your Roth. If you are in a lower tax bracket than you will be when you retire, then think about contributing to your Roth. *For example, if Annie is in school and working a part time job, then she is probably in a lower tax bracket than she will be when she retires. Thus, if she is able to save for retirement, she should use a Roth. On the other hand, if she is earning a professional salary, she is probably in a higher tax bracket, and her retirement savings would be more efficiently invested in a traditional IRA.*

One more quick thought: when you pay a tax now, the transaction with the government is done, and the money is out of your control. If you "kick the can down the road" and pay the tax later (like with a traditional IRA), then there is always a possibility that you can figure out a great strategy to not pay that tax, such as the qualified charitable distribution we just discussed.

That said, here's a clever thing you can do with a Roth IRA: You have already paid tax on the money you contributed to a Roth IRA, so you can take it back out of the account at any time. The earnings on your "contributions" (the money you put into the account) can only be taken out under some strict circumstances: typically only after the account has been open for 5 years, and after you turn 59.5 years old. There are also provisions for using the earnings for medical expenses and for $10,000 to buy a house, but a better idea allows you to save for that house without taking out any earnings, and thus not paying tax on any withdrawals. With most retirement accounts, you will get hit with taxes and penalties if you take any money out before retirement age. The penalties can be steep. With a Roth IRA, as long as you only withdraw the contributions, you don't have any taxes or penalties at all.

Let's say you want to save for a down payment on a house, but you also want to save for retirement. You want to target having $20,000 for a down payment in five years, but you figure you will want to start saving next year, after you get these credit cards paid off. Here's one thing you can do:

Year 1. Open a Roth IRA with $50.
Year 2. Put $5k in your Roth.
Year 3. Put $5k in your Roth.
Year 4. Put $5k in your Roth.
Year 5. Put $5k in your Roth.

The "Not a Tax Book" Tax Book

Don't Go There Doug!
Doug converted a 401(k) into his five year old Roth by rolling it over and paying tax on the conversion. Then he withdrew the contributions in order to buy a house boat, because he has always dreamed of sailing around the keys. Don't go there, Doug! If you roll funds into a Roth those funds have to be in the account for five years before you can withdraw the contributions penalty free. There are multiple "five year rules," and they can get confusing, so talk to your tax professional before making any withdrawals.

Ok, it has been five years, and you have contributed $20,050. If your money grew at ~8% your account balance will be around $23k, which is the $20k you contributed and $3k or so of growth. Now you can take out your $20k for the down payment (tax if and penalty free) and you still have that extra $3k in the Roth IRA that can continue to grow, tax free, until you need it after you retire.

Hot Tax Tip
Open a Roth IRA today to get the five-year clock started. Many brokerage firms will allow you to start one with as little as a dollar.

Another reason for this idea is that your account has to be open for 5 years before you take out any earnings - even after you reach retirement age! In other words, let's say you are 58.5 years old and you establish a Roth IRA. You put in $7,000. The next year you're 59.5 (the age to take out Roth IRA earnings without penalty), and your account has grown to $8,000. You can take back the original $7,000, but you have to wait four more years to take out the earnings! However, if you established the account 5 years ago, even if you only put $1 in it to begin with, then you contributed the $7,000 at age 58.5 like we mentioned before, you can take the entire $8,000 out as soon as you turn 59.5 because the account is over 5 years old.

> **Questions for your tax professional:**
> 1. Can I take out Roth contributions the same as cash rolled into my Roth?
> 2. What is a "backdoor Roth" conversion?
> 3. What are the Roth contribution limits based on my age?

Zoë's Backdoor Roth

Tax savings potential: $$

Key topics in this story:
Tax
- How a backdoor Roth IRA works.
- Why would anyone want to try a backdoor Roth?

Two tax pros are sitting in a bar, when one says to the other, "Ever handle a backdoor Roth?" Is that a funny joke? No, to be honest it doesn't even make sense. Does "backdoor Roth" sound like it might be part of a joke? Yes.

We have a client named Zoë, and she's an actuary. She makes a lot of money, because while most people avoided statistics class, she loved it, she's really good at it, and she spent many years studying statistics and mathematics. In any case, her high income means she doesn't get to take a deduction for an IRA contribution, and she can't contribute directly to a Roth IRA at all. She has her 401(k) totally maxed out every year, but she still has cash that she would like to invest for retirement. She's in a pretty good position, financially-speaking.

Of course, Zoë can make a contribution to a regular IRA, but she doesn't get a deduction for it. If she does contribute to a non-deductible IRA, the money she puts in the account grows tax free until she retires, and she has to keep careful track of how much she has contributed and file special forms every year (because when she withdraws the funds she pays tax on the gains in the account, but not on the original contribution). It's called a "non-deductible IRA." Does that sound overly complex, to the point that you wouldn't want to even mess with it? If so, you're in good company.

Zoë is really good at math, so she's not afraid of the calculations and the record keeping, but she's also really smart, and she knows a way to skip all of that and simply not pay tax on any of the money she withdraws from her non-deductible IRA when she retires. It's called a backdoor Roth. With our help, Zoë realized that, even though she makes too much money to contribute to a Roth IRA, there is no income limit when it comes to converting regular IRA funds to a Roth IRA. Anyone can do it! All they have to do is pay the tax on any money being converted, and then the funds get the Roth IRA tax treatment, which is no tax at all.

Since Zoë is contributing non-deductible IRA funds, she already paid the tax on those contributions. Thus, there is no tax to pay when she converts to a Roth. Basically, it's a way for high-income people to make a Roth IRA contribution by filling out a simple form.

Making the backdoor Roth contribution is just as easy as making any other IRA contribution, which is to say it simply requires depositing the funds in an account and then instructing the brokerage firm to convert the funds to a Roth. It can all be done the same day!

There are a few "gotchas" with this strategy, so be sure you talk to your tax pro (in a bar?) before you make any plans for your backdoor Roth IRA. The most important one is that every contribution to your backdoor Roth has to be in the account for five years. (Otherwise, there is a 10% penalty).

Michael A. York, EA
Andrew L. Stevens, EA, MBA

> ### Don't go there Doug!
> Doug has several IRAs, and he also has a 401(k) through his work. He wants to make a backdoor Roth contribution, so he deposits the maximum in a new IRA and immediately converts it to a Roth. Don't go there, Doug! If you have existing IRAs, then aggregation rules apply: you won't get the full benefit of the backdoor Roth, and you will still be stuck with filing special forms to track your non-deductible IRA contributions. A backdoor Roth might still be a great idea for you, but it makes sense to talk to a tax professional first.

Now, we're not the biggest fans of Roths, especially for high-income people like Zoë. In her case, she has maxed out her other retirement savings options and she still wants to put more money away. For Zoë, a backdoor Roth is a great option to save additional funds for retirement.

It gets even better. If Zoë had simply left her non-deductible IRA in her IRA account without converting to the backdoor Roth, then when she turned 72 those funds would increase the amount of her RMDs (Required Minimum Distributions, discussed in detail in the chapter about Janet and Kyle), and thus increase her tax in retirement. But Roth IRAs don't count in the RMD calculation, so she can use that cash or leave it invested as she sees fit. By making the backdoor Roth conversion she gets tax-free growth, tax-free distributions, and she gains a ton of flexibility in retirement because she can choose which account to withdraw from, depending on her future needs.

But what if she wants to use that money before retirement? Easy! An example:

Zoë loves koala bears, and recently (before she retired) she saw that there was a fire in Australia that wiped out a big patch of koala habitat. If she wants to use some funds from her backdoor Roth to help the koalas, she can take any funds that have been in the account for five years, withdraw the amount she converted, and immediately send it to her favorite koala organization! In other words, if she contributed $5,000 five years ago, then converted it to a backdoor Roth on the same day, and it's worth $7,000 now, then she can take out the original $5,000 tax- and penalty- free and use it to save koalas. On top of that, the $2,000 that represents the growth in the account can continue to grow and be available, tax free when she retires!

> **Questions for your tax professional:**
> 1. What is a "backdoor Roth" conversion?
> 2. What are the Roth contribution limits based on my income?
> 3. How long do I have to wait before I can take money out of my backdoor Roth?
> 4. What are all the "five year" rules when it comes to Roth IRAs?

Kris' Roth Savings Account

Tax savings potential: $$

Key topics in this story:
Tax

- How to create a Roth savings account.
- What is the proper order for spending money out of retirement accounts to save taxes?

You learned about how Glenn gets a deduction for charitable contributions even without a Schedule A. Glenn's wife, Kris, does the same, and she also takes advantage of the fact that there is no age limit for contributions to Roth IRAs. *NOTE: As of 12/31/2019 there is also no age limit for regular IRA contributions!*

Kris works part-time, and her annual compensation is about $6,000, which is great because at any age a contribution to a Roth or other IRA requires compensation or profits from a business. Sadly, it's the case that pensions, dividends, interest, retirement benefits, social security, et al, don't count as compensation for making an IRA contribution. The only compensation that does count is money you get paid for working, or alimony.

> ### Hot Tax Tip
> You can basically use a Roth as a savings account as long as it has been open for 5 years, you're over retirement age, and you have compensation.

Kris could choose to put this money in any old savings account, checking account, mutual fund, or whatever. The key is, all of those pay interest or dividends, and those earnings are taxable. Why pay tax if you don't have to? Because there are no age restrictions on Roth IRA contributions, Kris can deposit her checks into her Roth account, and any earnings are tax free. Of course, Kris set up this Roth account ages ago, so she has passed the five-year test we discussed in another story, where a Roth account has to be at least five years old before the earnings can come out tax free.

> ### Don't Go There Doug!
> Doug wants a Roth savings account, but he's retired and all of his income comes from Social Security, IRA distributions, and interest and dividends from his investments. Don't go there, Doug! You can only contribute *earned* income to a Roth IRA.

Glenn and Kris are over 70 years old, so their money is invested conservatively, and they use funds from taxed accounts before touching funds from tax free accounts. They also save investment accounts for last. In other words, if Kris needs to transfer money into her checking account, she starts with accounts earning *taxable* interest. She draws down those accounts first, because they earn interest like her Roth, but that interest is taxable, while the cash in the Roth grows tax free. When and if those funds are depleted, then she draws from her Roth IRA account. Finally, she has money in some conservative investment accounts that will require that she pays capital gains tax if she liquidates any holdings. She takes that money last to avoid paying capital gains tax, and because if she happens to pass away before she needs the money in those accounts, her heirs will get a "step up" in basis, which will wipe out any capital gains tax that Kris would have had to pay had she used that money.

Questions for your tax professional:
1. In what order should I take money out of my retirement plans?
2. Do I have compensation required to contribute to a Roth IRA?

Allene bunches deductions every other year for big savings

Tax savings potential: $$$

Key topics in this story:
Tax

- Bunch charitable contributions to maximize tax savings.
- Use the enhanced standard deduction to save extra taxes in "off" years.

A key aspect of the Tax Cuts and Jobs act is the increase in the standard deduction, which for 2019 is $12,200 for single people and $24,400 for married taxpayers. The increase was meant to offset some reductions in key deductions, such as state and local income taxes. Our friend Allene's Schedule A has $10,000 in state and local taxes (SALT), about $10,000 in mortgage interest, and every year she makes about $5,000 in charitable contributions. Added up, that's about $25,000 per year in Schedule A itemized deductions, which is just a hair over the standard deduction. In other words, from all of her deductions, she's just barely better off itemizing rather than taking the standard deduction.

Allene used to make her donation every December, but on even years she waits until January, which is just a week past when she would normally make the contribution. No big deal, right? Well let's look at how it works out for tax purposes. In odd years, she takes the standard deduction, which is $24,400. In even years, she takes a deduction of 30,000, because of the $5,000 contribution in January and the $5,000 contribution in December.

If Allene had simply taken her regular itemized deduction of $25,000 every year, it would have given her a deduction of $50,000 over two years. At 24% federal income tax and 6% state, that's a tax savings of $15,000. However, by using the standard deduction one year and bunching her charitable contributions the next it gives her a deduction of $24,400 and $30,000, respectively, or $54,400 over two years, which gives her a nice savings of $16,320, which is a $1,320 improvement!

This is a pretty easy one to calculate. The key is that in years where you don't bunch charitable contributions, you use the standard deduction. If that's the case for you, then the larger your charitable contributions, the more you save!

Don't Go There Doug!
Doug wants to bunch everything! He neglects paying his property tax until January so he can bunch two years of property taxes, thinking it's going to help him save taxes (just like bunching charitable contributions). Don't go there, Doug! Bunching only works with certain expenses. Property taxes have their own rules about what year they can be deducted (not to mention the SALT limits that are mentioned above).

Questions for your tax professional:
1. If I bunch two years of charitable contributions, can I use the standard deduction in the off years?
2. Are there any other Schedule A deductions that I can bunch between years?
3. If I claim the standard deduction, will I actually be better off because my state refund won't be taxable?

Janet and Kyle use the Tax Cuts and Jobs Act to minimize retirement taxes

Tax savings potential: $$$$

Key topics in this story:
Tax
- Use the "enhanced" standard deduction to take tax-free money from your IRA.
- Lower your IRA account values to make your RMDs smaller and save money EVERY YEAR!
- Lower your RMDs, lower the amount of Social Security you get taxed on: a double tax savings.
- Use the standard deduction to move IRA funds to Roth IRA: tax free.

The standard deduction for a married couple went from $12,700 in 2017 to $24,000 in 2018. A couple we know retired this year, and their names are Janet and Kyle, and they're 62 years old. Janet and Kyle have some money in savings, plus some investment accounts, and of course they have a couple of big fat IRA accounts that they rolled their 401(k) accounts into when they retired. For at least a few years Janet and Kyle will be paying bills from their savings accounts and from liquidating long-term investments in order to minimize their tax bill, because anything that comes out of their IRAs is taxed as regular old income.

Michael A. York, EA
Andrew L. Stevens, EA, MBA

At age 70.5 (or 72 if your date of birth falls after July 1, 1949), everyone must start taking "required minimum distributions" from their Traditional IRAs (not Roths, for now). At that point, it's pretty much impossible to avoid paying income tax on that money. However, using the new standard deduction amount, there is a way to avoid some of that tax. Here's how Janet and Kyle do it.

For year 2019 their taxable income will be close to zero. That means they have $24,400 of "room" from the standard deduction they can use to shield themselves from taxes. How? By moving money from IRAs to savings accounts they will reduce the amount of required minimum distributions they will have to take in the future. Let's look at some numbers:

Year	Taxable Income	Estimated Std. Deduction	"Buffer"
2019	$500	$24,400	$23,900
2020	$3,500	$24,800	$21,300
2021	$5,000	$25,200	$20,200
2022	$7,500	$28,200	$20,700
2023	$8,000	$28,600	$20,600

The buffer represents the amount of money they can move from their IRAs into savings accounts every year without paying a cent of taxes on the distributions. This is money they can live on or save as necessary. "But why would they want to move money out of their IRAs? I thought the benefit of these accounts is tax free growth?" That is the benefit, but the detriment is that the year Janet and Kyle turn 72 years old they're required to start taking out "Required Minimum Distributions," or RMDs.

RMDs are designed to make the account owner draw down (and pay taxes) on IRA funds during their lifetime. Thus, the benefit of tax free growth starts to go away once the account holder turns 72 years old, and it might be better to transfer that money out of the IRA in order to shrink the RMDs, and thus pay less tax on the IRA proceeds. To use a simplified example, if the year they turn 72 years old they have IRAs totaling $1,000,000, their combined RMD would be $51,282. By using the "buffer" above, they could reduce their total IRAs to $893,300, which makes their RMD $45,810, a difference of $5,472. The tax on that $5,472 would have been $657, which means they saved $657 in tax for the first year of RMDs, and a greater amount than that every year after.

> ### Hot Tax Tip
> Use the standard deduction to get cash out of IRAs before you have to take RMDs. Reducing future RMDs can mean less retirement money taxed AND less Social Security benefits taxed.

But it gets even better than that. Up to 85% of Social Security benefits can be taxed like regular income, but the amount of Social Security that gets taxed is dependent on how much other income a taxpayer receives. By lowering their IRA account values and thus lowering their RMDs, Janet and Kyle also lowered the amount of their social security that gets taxed from 85% to 80%, which saved an additional several hundred dollars.

Finally, let's not forget the big prize here, which is the $106,700 that Kyle and Janet were able to move out of their IRAs, tax free. At the 12% tax bracket, that's a savings of $12,804!

Now, Janet and Kyle needed the cash from their IRA "buffer" distributions to live on, but what if they didn't? What if they had enough savings and other resources to avoid spending their IRA distributions for five years? Janet and Kyle could have used the "buffer" above to convert that amount of money from IRA to Roth IRA. We're not the biggest Roth IRA fans, but in this case a Roth makes sense. The only hiccup is that if you convert IRA money to Roth IRA, you have to wait five years before you can withdraw that money, but the nice thing is that you can make a Roth IRA contribution at any age (unlike a traditional IRA) as long as you have compensation.

Michael A. York, EA
Andrew L. Stevens, EA, MBA

> *Don't go there Doug!*
> Doug wants to take advantage of the standard deduction to move IRA money into savings accounts, but he doesn't want to go through the headache of carefully estimating his income for the year. He simply "ballparks" an amount to withdraw from his IRA. Don't go there, Doug! Without knowing exactly how much to withdraw, Doug can very easily take too much from his IRA, which would cause him to pay more tax than necessary *and* might have additional effects, like making him pay tax on a higher percentage of his Social Security benefits.

Let's look at a sample year from the example above. In 2019 Janet and Kyle had a "buffer" of $23,900 that they could use to take money out of their IRAs. Remember, money that comes out of an IRA is taxable as regular income, and money that comes out of a Roth IRA is tax free. If Janet and Kyle have a $23,900 buffer before they have to pay tax on any money that comes out of their IRA, here is what they do: Convert $23,900 from an IRA to a Roth, and report that as income on their tax return. The standard deduction wipes out the tax, and now they have $23,900 in a Roth they can use after five years, or they can let sit in the account. Either way, it's tax free when they need it. In this case, a Roth is better than a savings account because any interest or dividends it earns are totally tax free.

Just remember that Roth IRAs have to be open for five years before you can take penalty-free withdrawals of earnings, and money converted from IRA to Roth IRA has to sit in the account for five years before it can be withdrawn without a penalty. Janet and Kyle planned for this by opening their Roth account years ago, and they have worked with a financial planner to ensure they won't need the $24K they just converted from IRA to Roth for another five years, at least.

Questions for your tax professional:
1. When do I need to start taking required minimum distributions?
2. How much is my RMD, and how much will I be taxed on it?
3. Do I have a "buffer" to transfer money out of IRAs to lower my future RMDs?
4. Can you calculate my taxable social security benefits and show how reducing RMDs will reduce tax on my social security?

Hannah's kid's college fund bought a beach house

Tax savings potential: $$$$

Key topics in this story:
Tax
- How to invest for college with security and flexibility.
- How to invest in real estate with tax-free college savings funds.

Imagine a way to save for college that would allow the money to grow tax free and will still be tax free when it's used to pay for college expenses. If your kid doesn't go to college, this money can be transferred among other siblings and even cousins. This money can even be used to pay for private elementary through high school education. Most important: **you** control the funds! If your kiddo decides thewy would rather take their college fund and hang out at a coffee shop in Amsterdam until the money runs dry, you can say: "Nope!"

Michael A. York, EA
Andrew L. Stevens, EA, MBA

This is a real thing, and it's called a 529 Plan. It's named after a section of the tax code, which is always the sexiest way to name anything. (Side note: why even pass legislation to create great programs if you're not going to give them enticing names? Who is in charge of marketing this stuff?) Even though there isn't a federal tax deduction for putting money into a 529 plan, the plans are administered by each state. Some states offer tax breaks, so talk to your tax advisor.

> <u>Hot Tax Tip</u>
> Many states give tax breaks for contributing to a 529 plan. Don't let your financial advisor put your money into one of these plans without talking to your tax professional about any applicable tax savings.

Even if you don't know much about investing, you can probably set up and fund a 529 plan from the comfort of your living room in about ten minutes: they're that easy. In fact, one of the authors set up 529 plans for each of his nieces and nephews. Instead of giving them birthday and Christmas gifts every year (which would get lost in the sea of other gifts they receive), he puts money in their 529 plans. It may not be sexy now, but someday it'll blow their pants off.

Ok, so other than this being a great way to save for college, what is the big strategy here? For college, you can pay for the following expenses out of a 529 plan (tax free): Tuition and fees, books and supplies, computers and related expenses (internet), room and board, and special needs equipment. Now let's look at room and board more closely. You're probably thinking 529 money can only be used to pay for on-campus dorm rooms and meal plans, right? Nope.

Each college has to report a "cost of attendance" figure every year, and those numbers are very easy to find online. The national average runs about $10k for room and board. Harvard is toward the high end at $17k, and smaller state schools tend to run around $8k per year. You can spend up to the "cost of attendance" figure for your child's room and board with 529 funds, totally tax free.

> ### Don't Go There Doug!
> Doug rents a room to his daughter, a college student. She has roommates who pay fair market value for their rent. Doug charges his daughter less in order to budget more money for a new smart phone. Don't go there, Doug! Charging less than fair market value makes Doug's daughter's occupancy the same as Doug's occupancy, and Doug's rental property just lost a lot of the tax deductions that made it an attractive investment in the first place.

Ok, so what is the tax strategy? If your kid rents a room off campus, he or she is going to have a landlord, right? Why not have it be you? We've written a lot about residential real estate elsewhere in this book, so we won't go deep on the ins and outs of it here, but here is the gist: You purchase a property near the university, maybe a condo or a townhouse. Maybe it's big enough for your child and two roommates. The roommates would pay you rent, and here's the kicker: *You can pay yourself rent,* with money from your child's 529 plan.

Before anyone accuses us of coming up with some strategy to steal money from their children's college fund, that's not what we're doing here. The fact is, if your child goes to college they will need a place to live, and you might choose to pay for that place out of their college savings fund. That money can go to some shady landlord, or it could go back in your pocket.

Let's look at an example: Hannah's son was eight years old, and she started saving $10k per year for his college via a 529 account. When it was time for him to go to college, she had been saving for ten years in an account that earned some interest and dividends, and also had some growth of the investments. With $10k of contributions and averaging 9% growth every year, the account was worth $165k after ten years.

Hannah had considered using mutual funds to save for her son's college, and if she had, after paying taxes every year on interest and dividends, the fund would be worth about $163k after ten years.

> ### Records Check
> In this example Hannah is renting to a family member, so her records must be perfect, otherwise the IRS can say her son's days spent in the home are the same as Hannah living in the home, and thus none of her

Now, that's not a big difference, but when the funds come out of a 529 plan for college, they are tax free. When the funds come out of the other investment account they get hit with 15% long-term capital gains tax, so the real value of the non-529 account isn't $163k, it's really $138k. That's a difference of about $25k!

Back to this real estate idea. Instead of paying the university to house her son in a dorm or giving the rent to some slumlord that owns a big apartment complex near the university, Hannah bought a condominium near campus. She pays herself rent, and also collects rent from her son's roommate, which pays for the mortgage on the condo. Instead of the college fund cash going to some landlord, Hannah puts it aside for the day when her son calls her to tell her that his study-abroad program includes three weeks in Ibiza, and can he please borrow $10k for… food, because food is really expensive in the Mediterranean (or something).

One disclaimer: All of our disclaimers are about talking to a tax professional, but we'll add a little extra to this one. Renting to family members can be fraught with peril. You have to be extra careful, otherwise the IRS can count their use as your own "personal use" and throw out all of your deductions. There are a few rules, but the most important ones are that your child uses the property as their principal residence, and that you charge fair market rent (with proof and lots of documentation, of course).

You might be wondering, "Ok, so I bought a condo for my kid to live in while in college, but after four years (five), then what? I have an empty condo with college kid gunk all over it." We have some ideas. First, as a landlord, you could use security deposits from your renters (including your child) to clean the place up. Either keep the place as an investment property, or trade it, tax free, for another. Maybe you have another child going to school at another university – you could trade the first condo for another piece of real estate at your second child's school. You could also trade the condo for an investment property at a sunny vacation destination. Did we just suggest that in a roundabout way you could use college savings money to invest in a beach house? Yes! Is that unethical? No! In our opinion, it would be more unethical to give the money to some fat cat real estate investment trust (REIT) managers who would then use your child's college fund to purchase their *own* vacation homes.

For a deeper look at rental real estate, take a look at "Long-Term Linda" elsewhere in this book.

Questions for your tax professional:
1. What is fair rent for a college apartment for my kiddo?
2. Does my state offer a 529 plan and are there tax benefits for investing in it?
3. What if my kiddo doesn't go to college?
4. How can I roll the funds in my 529 to another person in the family?

Collin's awesome tip about Health Savings Accounts

Tax savings potential: $$$

Key topics in this story:
Tax

Michael A. York, EA
Andrew L. Stevens, EA, MBA

- Health savings accounts: flexible and tax-free savings accounts.
- How to use tax-free HSA funds to pay for anything you want.
- How to "save" medical receipts and cash them in on a rainy day.

A Health Savings Account (HSA) is a plan offered by many employers, plus third-party administrators who offer plans to self-employed people, as well as wage earners who don't have a plan through their work. HSAs allow you to receive a tax deduction for contributing up to $3,500 per year to an account that is designed to pay for medical expenses. For most people, that means they save $3,500 every year, then they pay for health insurance deductibles, prescription medicines, birth control, co-pays, vaccinations, and more with the money in their HSA. Most people actually *try* to spend every cent every year, because people confuse these with "flexible" spending accounts where people understand them to be "use it or lose it" accounts.

Before we dive into Collin's strategy, let's first talk about an uncommon fact about HSAs: you can save up your receipts and "cash them in" in future years. In other words, there's no problem with taking money out of your HSA in 2026 to reimburse yourself for an expense from 2019, as long as you have the receipts, and the expense was incurred in a year when you had an HSA. In other words, receipts from previous years, before you had an HSA don't count.

> <u>Hot Tax Tip</u>
> Save up those medical expense receipts and "cash" them in to your HSA only when you absolutely need to. Let that HSA money grow tax free as long as possible!

Back to Collin. Our friend contributes the maximum amount to his HSA every year, but he pays for his medical expenses out of pocket and doesn't reimburse himself out of his HSA. It sounds crazy, doesn't it? Well, here's the method behind his madness: Collin saves his receipts in an envelope, and he writes the total dollar amount of the receipts and the date range on each envelope. Meanwhile his HSA account grows tax free, with compounding interest and earnings.

> ### Records Check
> Be sure to record whether a given receipt has been reimbursed by the HSA or not - it's easy to get confused, and you don't want submit the same receipt twice!

A good general rule is to avoid withdrawing money from funds growing tax free, because the tax-free status allows for faster growth compared to other investments earning similar returns. By leaving his HSA money alone, Collin lets that money grow and grow and grow. But why? Well, sure, Collin could chip away at the funds with a $20 co-pay here and there, but he can afford these payments out of pocket (and he saves the receipts in case he wants to reimburse himself later). However, health care costs tend to get more expensive, and we need more care as we get older. By letting the funds grow, he's saving up a big nest egg that can be withdrawn tax free if he has a need for future medical expenses.

> ### Don't go there Doug!
> Doug never chose an investment for his HSA funds, and thus his account never earns interest and dividends. Don't go there, Doug! This strategy is all about allowing the fund to grow, tax free. Some of the account should be in cash, but otherwise if you plan to let the fund grow for years and years in order to get the maximum benefit from tax free growth, be sure to choose an appropriate investment allocation!

However, what if Collin has an unexpected expense in the meantime, like his car breaks down, and he doesn't have cash on hand to pay for it? Well, Collin simply withdraws from his HSA account an amount equal to some receipts from years past. He finds receipts that total the amount he needs, and he submits copies of them to the HSA administrator. Then he withdraws HSA funds in the amount of the receipts, and he marks them with "REIMBURSED" and the date so he doesn't accidentally double dip in the future. The money he withdraws from his HSA isn't taxed, because it's used to reimburse him for medical expenses (even though those expenses might have been from ages ago). Meanwhile, his HSA account benefited from tax free growth in the intervening years.

It gets even better. What if Collin's account grows and grows, and eventually he uses up all of his old receipts, but his account still has money in it? Collin can continue to draw from the account with new receipts, but what if we're 40 years into the future and medicine is practiced by robots and it's free and no one even gets sick anymore (then why do we need the robot doctors? This is why we don't write science fiction). Once Collin turns 65, he can use the funds in his HSA for anything he wishes without penalty. His HSA has, through the magic of the tax code, turned into a regular old retirement account. Isn't that great? An HSA is a tax free savings account, a great way to save for future medical expenses tax free, *and* it's a retirement savings vehicle. HSAs are so great we can hardly believe they exist at all. But what if you start using an HSA, and after a few years the rules change, or you simply decide you would rather use a different method of saving for future medical expenses? That's easy! Just cash in all of your old saved-up medical receipts and take your money, with no tax or penalties whatsoever.

Records Check
Sometimes receipts can fade with age. It couldn't hurt to scan the medical receipts you plan to save so that they can still be read years into the future.

Questions for your tax professional:
1. What are options for investing in an HSA either through my company, as a self-employed person, or through a third party administrator?
2. What documentation do you need to accurately report my HSA distributions as non-taxable?
3. Can I withdraw funds from my HSA any time I want to?

Michael A. York, EA
Andrew L. Stevens, EA, MBA

Section Five – All the Info You Still Need to Know

How to find a good tax professional

Do you need a tax professional? We think so! You may be considering going it alone and maybe using popular tax software to handle your tax preparation needs. Let us take a minute of your time to persuade you to use a professional instead.

We like to compare taxes to mountain climbing. If you're climbing a small hill you can surely do it on your own, but as you take on bigger mountains it begins to make sense to hire a professional to help you. With taxes, if your return is simple and you don't want to complicate your life by taking on tax savings strategies, you can probably do your return on your own with no issues. However, if you want to spend less money on taxes (we could be talking about thousands of dollars here!), it makes sense to hire someone to help you. The professional you hire knows the pitfalls and the shortcuts, and he or she can help you achieve your goals while helping navigate any risky sections. And let's not forget that even small hills can have unexpected obstacles and dangers. When it comes to taxes, in our experience, even on simple returns there are often complications that arise every so often that require a professional. Even with simple returns, we often see a situation every few years that allows us to help our client save significant money they would have lost, and in those instances our fee is less than the savings that would have been missed.

"Won't a tax professional simply ask all the same questions and fill out the same forms as my tax software?" The answer is: no. Tax software isn't prepared to handle gray areas, and tax law is full of gray areas. Also, tax software is rear-facing: It only asks what happened during the previous year. It doesn't ask about what you hope to achieve next year and then help you get there. Our mentor, Gary, used to say, "A good tax professional's job is to consider if we can turn a tax 'no' into a tax 'yes.'" What he meant was that we should be strategizing on behalf of our clients to make the tax code work for them, instead of simply telling them they can or can't do something (which is what software does).

Tax preparation is a big business. You've probably seen little cubicles set up in malls during tax time, or maybe you've seen a sad kid wearing a costume, twirling a sign in front of a strip mall from February to April. There are internet-based tax prep services that will electronically file your returns after they prepare them, and of course there are professionals who sit behind a desk and can answer your questions year-round. The fact is, there is no shortage of services available to help you file your taxes.

The question is, how do you know you're going to someone worth paying for his or her services? How do you know you're being given the right options to consider? One thing you can do is to gather up all of your documentation and visit a bunch of tax preparers in your area. You will spend a few hours with each, and whether you hire them or not, you will pay them for their time. If you're willing to spend hours and hours of time and several hundred dollars screening these tax preparers, you might find someone who will do a good job. Wait, that sounds like a total waste. Don't do that. Let's find a better solution.

Don't Go There Doug!
Doug has an initial consultation with a tax professional where they agree to work with each other in the next tax season. In the meantime, Doug sends his new tax professional plenty of emails, calls frequently, and expects all of the pre-work to be free, simply because he's paying a few hundred dollars for his tax return. Don't go there, Doug! If you are able to find a great tax pro who is around to answer your questions year-round, expect to pay a fair rate for their time. If you get great advice, you'll save more than you pay!

Michael A. York, EA
Andrew L. Stevens, EA, MBA

Let's look at the types of tax preparers. The first one is what we call a "buddy." It's just any random person who will help you, maybe for money, or maybe because you helped them fix their car. Unlike many professions, there is no law that says that you can't hire any old random person off the street to help you prepare your tax return. Generally speaking, we don't recommend having any old untrained "buddy" do your taxes, though his fee will probably be quite affordable. If you visit someone in a superstore kiosk, you might be getting a well-seasoned professional, but you might also be getting someone who passed a training course last Friday. Before you hand them your documents you might consider inquiring as to their level of experience.

Another thing to consider is whether your preparer can help represent you before the IRS if you happen to get audited. Even though anyone can prepare a tax return, there are only three types of tax professionals who can represent you before the IRS. In other words, your buddy might be able to fill out the forms, but if you get audited they're not allowed to represent you on their own. The three professions who are designated to represent you before the IRS are: a) an enrolled agent, b) a certified public accountant, and c) an attorney.

What's the difference? Attorneys go to law school, pass the state bar exam, and some choose to specialize in taxation. Certified Public Accountant (CPA) is a title bestowed on people who have passed their state's CPA exam, which includes some material on taxation. The test also covers "attest" work, financial reporting issues, and more. An EA is a nationally-recognized designation that means someone has passed a three-part exam that covers the tax code and nothing but the tax code, and it's the highest credential awarded for tax professionals by the IRS.

No matter which tax professional you choose, we recommend someone who values education and continued learning (after all, tax laws change all the time), someone who is eager to spend time to not just talk about your taxes from last year, but will also help you strategize for future tax scenarios, and finally, we recommend a tax professional who values getting to know you and your specific tax situation, sort of like a good physician who bases medical recommendations based on her intimate knowledge of your family, not just what the text book says.

When it comes to choosing a professional to help you with your taxes, we strongly recommend finding someone who is an EA, a CPA, or an attorney who specializes in tax preparation. As long as they have one of those designations, they have passed our first recommended filter. Of course, that's not the only filter we recommend. Plenty of tax preparers are very skilled at reviewing your information and accurately preparing your tax return, but you could be missing out on some big opportunities for tax savings if you only speak to them at your appointment in February (and our guess is you already have a bunch of questions you could ask them right now). A good tax person is busy all year long: They're either working on preparing tax returns, they're booked solid with tax planning appointments, or they're training to learn the new tax laws.

With that in mind, let's look at some questions you can ask prospective tax professionals before you commit.

Are you around all year to answer questions?

We appreciate it when our clients reach out with tax questions. We've never once felt like the question was embarrassing, or a waste of our time. Likewise, every single year there are a few situations where we say, "I wish you would have called me before you did this." There are many, many transactions that people get involved with that either end up costing them a lot of money, or creating a massive paperwork project that they have to pay us to clean up. We always prefer to counsel our clients on the right way to do things before they find themselves in a difficult position when they file their taxes.

Can you represent me before the IRS if I happen to get audited?

If you have a tax professional who isn't an EA, CPA, or attorney, their answer is going to be "no," but that's not necessarily a bad thing. Plenty of firms have specialists who handle all of their audit work, and plenty of other practitioners prefer to outsource audits to trusted partners. We include this question because it's a good idea to know your tax professional's approach to audits to make sure you understand the process beforehand. Make sure you understand any audit representation fees, travel fees, associate fees, et al, and make sure you take those costs into account when deciding to work with someone.

Michael A. York, EA
Andrew L. Stevens, EA, MBA

Do you offer year-end tax planning?

In our practices tax planning is a requirement for our clients who have businesses. December 31 is the hard cut off for almost anything you can do to save taxes for a given year, so a good tax professional will want to meet with you late in the year to go over your numbers and strategize some things you can do to help yourself before January 1.

Do you review previous tax returns?

Any good tax preparer would prefer to not do your current tax return without looking at previous tax returns. Examining a past return is helpful in case there are certain forms that you have forgotten, and there are frequently numbers that need to flow or "carry over" from one year to the next. There's another great reason your tax preparer would want to review previous tax returns: Frequently when we discover mistakes in a previous return, fixing them actually gives money back to the client. In cases when it doesn't give money back to the client, it at least allows us to correct things in a way that reduces the client's audit exposure. We haven't seen a situation where reviewing a past return has hurt a client, and in many cases it puts money back in their pocket and allows them to sleep better at night knowing their taxes were prepared correctly.

Do you proactively contact clients with ideas for their businesses?

Tax professionals are constantly learning new ideas (or they should be!), and when a lightbulb goes off in their heads with something that will benefit some of their clients, they should contact those clients as soon as possible. At the risk of generalizing, a lot of tax professionals are not outgoing to the point that they will pick up the phone and call their clients when they have a great idea. You might decide you want a tax professional who makes contact more frequently than once or twice per year.

Do you send out a newsletter?

If they aren't the type to pick up the phone, maybe they collect all of these ideas and send out a newsletter periodically. If so, you should ask to take a look at a recent one to see if it's simply an advertisement for services or if there are actually some great ideas and strategies contained in it. Of course, if they don't have a newsletter that's ok as long as they're the type to call or email when inspiration strikes.

Do you have other clients with businesses similar to mine?

Depending on the particulars of your business you might want a tax professional who is experienced in that field. Not every business is so complicated that it needs a specialist tax pro, but it makes sense to discuss your business in great detail and ask if they work with clients who face similar issues. He or she should be able to talk to you about their clients and how they have helped them, which should give you an idea of their level of expertise with respect to your business.

Do you consider yourself aggressive or conservative?

What is the right answer to this one? We would say it depends on you! If you're aggressive by nature, you might want a conservative tax professional to reign you in a little. You might also want someone as aggressive as you, who shares your level of comfort with gray areas and ambiguity. It also might be a good idea to find someone who is aggressive on certain issues and conservative on others. It's really all about finding someone with the personality to fit your needs as a taxpayer.

What percentage of your business is tax returns?

Believe it or not, not all CPAs and tax attorneys are tax specialists. Plenty of CPAs spend 90% of their time doing audit or financial preparation, and plenty of tax attorneys spend most of their time doing estate planning, and then dabble in tax preparation during tax season in order to be a "one stop shop" for their clients (and to make a few extra bucks). We recommend a tax professional who focuses on taxes like a laser beam at all times, not one who starts thinking about taxes around the same time *you* do every year.

Likewise, it's ok to find a tax professional who "outsources" certain work like audit representation and tax resolution. We love specialists! Think about it, if you go to the doctor do you want them to tell you that they're the best family doctor and they can also fix that torn cartilage in your knee and they can help with seasonal depression and they can help you come up with a diet plan and they can tell whether that mole can come off or whether it needs to be biopsied? At a certain point that doctor sounds like they might be a quack! It could be a red flag if a prospective tax professional claims to be the ultimate expert on everything related to taxes. Of course, there are big firms out there that employ all manner of specialists, and if your professional works at one of these firms you're probably in good shape. Otherwise, don't be surprised if your tax professional refers you to a specialist from time to time if you need one.

Finally, talk to your friends and network with colleagues to find a tax professional you trust, and don't be afraid to change things up if your current tax professional isn't performing as you expect. They're not magicians, and if you bring them a mess in late March, you can't expect a miracle by mid-April. But if you can find someone who will work with you throughout the year and who is passionate about helping your business grow, you will be much better off.

Now that you've decided to start a business, where to begin?

Starting a business is such a daunting task with so many moving parts and so many seemingly insurmountable obstacles that many people give up before they even really start. We hope to de-mystify a lot of that so you don't get bogged down and frustrated by the whole process. We tackle such topics as permits and licenses: whether and how to get them. Offices: when should you consider moving out of your home office into a more professional space? If you already have some of the tools, equipment, merchandise, raw materials, and computers you need, how can you convert those to business assets and get a deduction for it? How can you figure out if you can make money from your idea (how to "model" a business)? And finally, maybe there are already competitors out there. How can you evaluate them and decide whether the timing is right for you to start your business?

Do you need permits or licenses?

The short answer is "maybe," but the more accurate short answer is "probably not." One myth we see a lot is this idea that anyone who starts a business needs some kind of all-encompassing "business license," sort of like how anyone who goes fishing needs a fishing license. If you are handling food or your business deals with anything that has a public health component, you likely need a permit or license. If you are leasing commercial space for your business, there is a good chance you will need an occupancy permit. Otherwise, if you are simply starting the business out of your home and not dealing with anything that might impact someone's health, you may not need a license; however, every location is different so check with your local government first. Almost every municipality in America has some kind of commerce board that is tasked with helping people get answers to these kinds of questions, and in many areas you can apply for just about anything you need online.

You may need to apply for a Federal Tax ID number (EIN number), a Doing Business As certificate (DBA), a sales tax certificate, and other documentation from your local government, but with online access you should be able to take care of everything yourself in about 30 minutes (maybe 45 if you're required to print, sign, and mail anything).

Do you need an office?

The short answer: yes! No matter what kind of business you run, you need some type of physical space where you conduct the "business" part of your daily activities. Even if your business has you in the car for your work day, you still need a place to store things, to do your bookkeeping, send out bills, open mail, make phone calls, and so on. Some people will need to lease space for an office, but most of us can make use of some space in our homes. If you've already decided that you need a home office, take a look in our "Other Useful Information" section for a pretty complete discussion of everything you need to know, including some myths about how the IRS seems to regard offices in the home.

> **Hot Tax Tip**
> There different ways to calculate a home office deduction, talk to your tax professional about which method benefits you the most.

If you're still on the fence, consider this: Every major corporation has a human resources function, a marketing function, a finance function, accounts payable and receivable, an executive group, salespeople, and information technology, to name just a few. When you run your own business, you need all of those functions as well. If you don't hire someone else to do that work, it's up to you to do it. Your office is where you sit down to get a lot of that stuff done. The point is, even if you don't do the money-making part of your business from an office, you probably still need one, and while it may not make financial sense to go out and lease a space, it very likely makes sense to convert part of your home into an office. (There is a pervasive myth that an office in the home an audit trigger, but we've dispelled that notion in the "Common Tax Misconceptions" section).

Competition: Is it good or bad?

You've done the math and constructed your business model, and maybe you have even written a business plan. Then you get online and search for people providing a similar service in your area, and there are dozens. Or maybe you search online for someone selling a similar product and find tons of results. Is it time to throw in the towel? After all, there are other people already doing what you're going to be doing, so how can you possibly build a business in the same industry where they are already established?

The fact is that there is always going to be competition, whether you join an existing industry as a newly established competitor, or if you invent your own industry and then are greeted with new competitors a few years down the line. Ultimately, competition is proof of concept. Here's what we mean by that: If the idea couldn't work, there wouldn't be businesses doing it. If there are businesses making money, then you can make money, too. Imagine going to a sophisticated investor with your business model and business plan in hand:

it's counter-intuitive, but in our experience that investor would rather see that you have a plan for how to operate better than established competitors than see that you have come up with an idea for a business that no one has ever thought of before.

You do need to be aware of market saturation, which is when there are too many businesses serving the same set of customers. However, it's pretty easy to calculate whether a market is saturated. You can do some back-of-the-envelope calculations based on the number of customers you need to be profitable, as identified in your business model, then compare that to the number of customers already being served in your area. Even easier than that is to start watching the market now, and if you see competitors dropping off, that's a good indication that the market is saturated. Even easier than that is to join some social media groups that are organized around your business and ask them about market saturation. You might wonder if people will be willing to share that information, but like many things that shouldn't be shared, it will likely end up posted on social media.

Hot Tax Tip
If there is a type of business, there is probably a social media group for that type of business. You can get more information than you can imagine by joining such a group and asking questions.

Another benefit of competition is that there are ready-made acquirers in your industry. Maybe you want to start a business and run it forever, but wouldn't it be great if you could sell the business if you wanted to? If you ever want to sell, a competitor is your most likely buyer - they already know the industry, they can add your business to theirs without developing a lot of new competencies, and it's an "easy" way to grow a business that doesn't involve starting from scratch. The flip side of that coin is that your competitors are also the first place to look if you want to grow your own business by acquiring someone else's. The point is: don't look for markets where no one is competing. Look for markets where there are competitors that you believe you can beat.

Michael A. York, EA
Andrew L. Stevens, EA, MBA

A note on pricing and price wars: The first place many new business people look for advantages over competition is price. They think if they just price a little lower than the competition, they can draw away customers, and thus win. What they neglect to consider is the obvious consequence, and that is the competitor might drop his prices as well. If this goes more than a round or two, you've found yourself in a price war, and no one wins a price war (except for maybe big box retailers circa 1999 and the handful of consumers who prioritize price over quality, service, convenience, expertise, and post-sale support). Think of price as the least attractive battlefield for your company's campaign against its competitors.

One more thing: In many markets your *com*petitors are really your *co*-petitors (if we may coin a new phrase). Certain businesses don't rely on repeat customers, and thus once a customer has visited them, it's not as likely they will come back. A great example is the trend of escape rooms (you and your friends are "locked" in a room with an immersive scenario, and you have to figure out how to escape). Once you have played through a scenario you know all the secrets, so it's not fun to play that one again. A business might have three or four scenarios, and once you have played them all, you're not going back to that location until they change their themes.

In a business like this you compete with similar businesses for customers, but there are actually many cooperative elements: One business that performs poorly might turn off customers, who then won't want to go experience what other businesses offer. On the flip side, if a new customer has an amazing experience they become "hooked" on the activity and want to visit all of the different versions they can. In a business like this, it makes sense to build a strong local community in order to improve everyone's offerings and thus improve customer experience (and likelihood of sharing those customers).

Another example is local theater. Once someone has seen a play, they typically don't go back over and over again (phenomena like *Hamilton* notwithstanding), but they may get bitten by the theater bug and want to go see other productions, which benefits other theater companies at least locally, if not nationally. This may not apply to your business at all, but it's something to think about if it seems like your venture is already loaded with potential competitors.

Common tax misconceptions

Cash doesn't have to be reported.

This one is incredibly common. Most people probably understand that if you earn money (even when paid in cash), you are required to pay tax on it. The disconnect arises when people think, "How will anyone know that I was paid in cash unless I report it?" That's a good question, and the IRS thinks it's a good question, too. They think about that one a lot, and they have come up with lots of creative ways to catch people who underreport income. A quick example of a creative "solution" to this issue is a cash-only pizza restaurant. The IRS is happy to examine bank records, but they can also simply look at how many pizza boxes the restaurant used during the year. If the restaurant used 5,000 pizza boxes, but claims they only sold 3,000 pizzas, you can bet the IRS is going to sauce all over the business with an order of back taxes owed, plus a side of penalties, and a large serving of interest.

You're not convinced? We had a new client, let's call him Jerry. Jerry was a teacher, and one summer before he first came to us he started a cash business that dealt with riding lawn mowers. He was an expert at fixing them, and he made a little money finding broken down mowers and refurbishing them. He paid cash and was paid in cash, and he didn't want to report the income.

"Jerry, does it cause you any stress to know that you will be in big trouble if the IRS finds out about this money?"

"Of course!"

Let's be honest with each other for a second. Even if you're never caught, you're going to lose at least a little sleep if you try to hide income from the IRS.

In the end, we coached Jerry on how to structure his riding mower activities as a real business. He started tracking his income and expenses like a real business, and we used legitimate strategies to help him reduce his tax burden. Jerry had losses some years and profit in others, but the most interesting part was this: We removed the stress he was feeling about not reporting income, and by running his business like a real business, wouldn't you know it, but his business actually improved. By doing all the things one does to prove a profit motive, Jerry improved his profits! His summer side hustle went from a little cash here and there to a full-year money maker, and Jerry sleeps like a baby knowing the IRS isn't going to take the money he rightfully earned.

Putting a sticker on your vehicle makes it an advertisement and thus every time you go somewhere it's deductible.

If we had a nickel for every time we've heard someone spout this or ask it in a meeting, we'd have over seven dollars. Do the math: that's a lot! If you're driving to drop your kids off at school, the IRS is never going to agree that you are driving for business. It doesn't matter what is on your car. You can deduct legitimate business use of your car, you can deduct the cost of the sticker or vehicle wrap, and that's it. At this point a lot of people go "Oh, never mind then." And we're like, "Wait, I thought this was a great advertising scheme. If it doesn't make every mile deductible, it's not worth it? What about the advertising benefits?" And then they say, "I'm not even sure I'd get that much business from it." And then we say, "That's why the IRS is on to this one."

The home office is an audit trigger.

This is another frequent misconception. Do you know how search engines chooses which websites show up first when you search for something? Neither do we. We know there is *some* kind of algorithm that generates search results, and there seem to be some things the algorithm prefers, and we know that the algorithm changes with some frequency. It's the same with an IRS audit, but add in random chance. Every tax professional will have some general theories about what might trigger an audit, just like every search engine optimization consultant will have some theories on how the algorithm works, but very few people know the real information. The home office is a perfectly acceptable and legal business deduction, but like any tax matter, there are rules. If you follow those rules and keep good records, you will be fine. Next year the audit trigger is international trust disbursements, anyway. (Wait, that's a secret. Don't tell anyone).

Real estate agents' hair and makeup expenses are deductible.

Sorry to pick on real estate agents, but they're an easy target on this one. For some reason their headshots are on their business cards. Why? Who chooses a real estate agent based on attractiveness? We could really spin out on a rant on this one, because buying and selling a house is the biggest financial transaction most people will enter in their entire lives, and yet for some reason people place importance on how their agent looks. It's bizarre. With all that said, we hear all the time that people in certain occupations get to deduct the cost of their hair and makeup and teeth whitening, because physical attractiveness is part of the job.

Unfortunately, the IRS and the tax courts have already ruled on this one, and hair, makeup, teeth whitening, and clothing aren't deductible expenses for most people. There are some rules about when clothing can be deductible, and they're pretty strict. In a nutshell, the clothing must be essential to the job (a nurse's uniform or a policeman's uniform, for example), it must not be suitable for wearing on the street (the uniforms above, plus things like an actor's stage costume or anything a magician wears), and finally, the clothing isn't worn outside of conducting business. When a police officer wakes up on a day off, he or she doesn't throw on the uniform and head to breakfast, because the uniform isn't appropriate for wearing off-duty. Likewise, an actor playing Hamlet doesn't throw on some tights and a codpiece and hit the town, nor does a surgeon wear scrubs to go to the mall. Wait, scratch that last one, they do that all the time, but we think it's for a specific reason. The only time hair and makeup would be deductible is if it's paid for by the taxpayer, it's required in order to perform the job (not simply preferred), it's not suitable for normal wear, and as a general rule it's not worn on the street. A good example is a television newscaster who purchases her own makeup. It's required to be worn, TV makeup looks weird on the street, and they typically wash it off before they leave the studio. If that doesn't sound like *your* job, then hair, makeup, teeth whitening, and clothing aren't deductible.

You have to make a profit for three years.

This one is kind of true, and kind of not true. We need to dive into the idea of an IRS "safe harbor" in order to understand it better. Because the laws are so confusing and ambiguous and constantly changing, the IRS has rules and guidelines, and they also have something called "safe harbors." In real life a safe harbor is a place you can anchor your boat where nothing bad will befall it, like typhoons, pirates, or tidal waves. In IRS-speak a safe harbor is an abstract way of saying, "if you do these things, you're good, we won't come after you." In other words, if your boat (business) is anchored in this safe harbor (follows these rules), then you have satisfied some IRS requirements, and you can sleep a little better.

One of the most famous (and least understood) of these safe harbors is the profit in three out of five years test. You will hear all the time "You *have* to make a profit in three out of five years." It's not true, but it's also not *not* true. Let's look into it. When it comes to part-time businesses and side hustles, the IRS is quite aware that some people will take a hobby and try to dress it up like a business in order to get extra tax benefits. There are a bunch of tests the IRS uses to determine if something is a hobby or a bona fide business, and one of them is whether or not the activity made money. In fact, if the activity made a profit in three out of the last five years, that is a "safe harbor," meaning in many cases the IRS will acknowledge that it's a business and not a hobby. The IRS doesn't have to stop there, but they do have to go to extra lengths to prove it's a hobby if this safe harbor is met. In rare cases, the IRS might still be able to prove it's a hobby, like if the business made a profit of $10 for three years, then had losses of $10K for two. In that case, they might be able to show that the business owner structured things to specifically meet the safe harbor requirements but was still engaged in something that was never going to be profitable, and is therefore just a hobby. Otherwise, if the safe harbor is met, the taxpayer is pretty much home free. You don't *have* to make a profit in three out of five years, it just gets you into the safe harbor. In fact, if you're breeding horses, the safe harbor is two out of seven years, and if you don't meet the safe harbor test at all, you may be able to easily pass some other tests to prove you are, in fact, in business. Let's look at those.

First, the IRS is going to look at whether or not you "carry on the activity in a businesslike manner." Let's compare two people who take pictures of sunsets: Hobby Harry and Business Betsy. Harry never put together a business plan, but Betsy did, and it outlines the steps she is going to take to make her photography business a money maker. Harry couldn't tell you how many miles he drove last year taking pictures of sunsets. He knows it was a lot, though; at least 60% of his miles. Betsy has a log of all the miles she drove taking pictures of sunsets. Harry doesn't have a separate business bank account for his income and expenses, but Betsy does. Harry made $5k selling his pictures online last year, but he couldn't show you exactly when and how much each picture sold for. On the other hand, Betsy also made $5k, and she has a spreadsheet showing exactly when each picture sold, to whom, and for how much money. Betsy is carrying on the activity in a businesslike manner, and she has a better chance of passing this test than Harry.

Next, the IRS will look at how much time and effort you put into the activity. Harry takes pictures when inspiration strikes him, or when he's on vacation, or sometimes he mixes it up and takes pictures of sunrises when his neighbor's illegal rooster wakes him up at dawn. Betsy, on the other hand, is systematic. She has a calendar she keeps of the prospective weather conditions and the exact time of the sunset and sunrise. She has her gear ready to go every day in case conditions are such that she can get a good shot. She took a class on photo processing in order to learn how to enhance her photos before she puts them on her website. Harry's time and effort is minimal, which makes his photography activity look more like a hobby he does in his spare time, and Betsy's time and effort go to showing that she is, in fact, running a business.

After that, the IRS will look at whether you depend on the income for your livelihood. This one is pretty self-explanatory, but let's just say that Harry is a trust fund kid, and Betsy intends to help make ends meet with her photography profits as soon as the business takes off. In this case Harry wouldn't pass the test and Betsy might.

If there are losses beyond your control, the IRS won't count those against you. In Harry's case, his website was down for four days due to a bot attack, and it cost him $4k to rebuild it. Harry simply says, "Hey, it wasn't my fault, man!" The same bots attacked Betsy's site, but she has records to document the expense, when it happened and why, and she even kept her email history with the developers who rebuilt her site, with all of the messages about their attempts to recover the site before opting for a full rebuild. In both cases the losses are outside of the control of the owner, but Betsy's losses are better documented and better demonstrate that the losses were something she couldn't have controlled.

One of the key things the IRS will look at is how you've changed things up to improve profitability. Harry buys a new camera every year before going to Hawaii to take pictures of sunsets on the beach at the same resort. He posts the pictures on his website, and he hasn't changed his prices at all since he started. Betsy, however, keeps track of what is selling and what isn't, and she works to take more of the types of pictures that sell. She has experimented with advertising on her site and other sources of revenue (like wedding photography and professional portraits), and she recently started a video channel to get exposure and hopefully make a few bucks. Most importantly, she keeps records of when and why she makes the decisions that she does. Harry hasn't changed things up in search of profits, which is exactly what hobbyists tend to do. Betsy, however, is far more businesslike in her quest for cash.

The IRS will also look at whether you have the knowledge needed to make a profit, or if you have advisors who have that knowledge, and also whether you have made a profit in similar activities in the past. Harry got into photography on a lark. He doesn't really know any other photographers, and if you put a photograph in front of him, he can't tell you what's good or bad about it. More importantly, if you ask him about how his business is similar to other successful photographers, he doesn't know enough about their businesses to give a complete answer. Betsy, however, is "friends" with successful photographers online, and she chats with them regularly and asks for advice. She has taken classes on photograph composition and lighting, and she has knowledge of the operations of a profitable photography business.

Finally, the IRS will examine whether you can expect a future profit from selling the assets in your business. Harry buys a new camera every year and sells his old one, always at a loss. Betsy, however, buys used cameras every year and holds them until they reach "vintage" status before selling them, and she tends to break even.

The IRS is quite holistic when it comes to examining whether something is a hobby or a business, and while there are "safe harbors" you can use to protect yourself, they're not a sure thing. Whether you qualify for a safe harbor or not, the best advice for any business is to *run it like a business.* If you do that, one of two things will happen: you will earn enough money to qualify for the safe harbor, or you will run your business in a way that will protect you even if you don't make money. Don't believe us? We told you about that guy who survived an audit after deducting expenses from trying to become a professional golfer (he wasn't successful, nor did he ever show significant profits). His books and records must have been pretty impressive, even if his short game never came around…

How to get organized and make sure you capture every deduction you deserve

One of our clients' biggest challenges is figuring out how to organize their tax records, and how to continue to organize them week after week and month after month. If that doesn't sound like you, then maybe you can skip this section. After all, there are plenty of extremely organized people who we're sure could teach us a lot of new tricks. This next bit is a simple guide for people who don't know where to start when it comes to getting organized and saving things like receipts. Whether you are extremely organized or you save important papers in a big pile, be sure to consult your tax professional on what records you should keep and for how long they need to be saved. Let's break down some tips and best practices.

First, get a dedicated business checking account with a debit or credit card. Use that card exclusively for business and try not to pay cash for anything. A separate bank account is one of the key things the IRS looks for when establishing whether you have a business or a hobby, so let's just assume that a separate bank account isn't just a good idea, it's the law (practically speaking).

Don't Go There Doug!
Doug bought football tickets with his business credit card. He figured it's all his money anyway, and he would simply correct the mistake using his bookkeeping software. Don't go there, Doug! If Doug had a regular job with a traditional employer, would that employer be ok with him charging personal expenses to his business credit card? No, they wouldn't, and the reason is obvious – the employer would be concerned about co-mingling funds, and the IRS is going to be concerned about that sort of thing as well.

Michael A. York, EA
Andrew L. Stevens, EA, MBA

Second, use QuickBooks or some other bookkeeping application to organize and balance your bank account. These programs see every transaction in your account, including the balance. Every time you make a purchase or pay a bill, it will show up in your bookkeeping program. Every few days simply log in and categorize each expense (this gets easier the more you do it: after a few times doing this most apps will learn which expenses go in what category). Keep in mind that at some point you may need to hire an actual bookkeeper. A good bookkeeper can actually improve your bottom line and help you make more money.

Third, the IRS likes to see backup documentation for expenses, which means receipts, receipts, receipts. Here's what we recommend: Take four big manila envelopes, and label *Jan-Mar*, *Apr-Jun*, *Jul-Sep*, and *Oct-Dec*, and of course label them with the current year. For most people this will be plenty of space, but if you have tons of receipts you might prefer to do monthly envelopes. Now put these envelopes (or at least the one you're currently using) somewhere really convenient, because your first stop after every work day is your envelope, where you empty your purse or your pockets to file your receipts. If your office is convenient, great. We like to keep a "holding" envelope in our car, and every time we make a business purchase we stick the receipt in the envelope. Every so often we transfer receipts from the car envelope to the main envelope in the house. If you get any documents in the mail, be sure to stuff them into your envelopes so they don't get lost.

Fourth, keep a tax journal. Many people keep theirs in the car most of the time. Every time they have a business meal or need to record some business expense (like parking paid in cash) they simply write it down in their journal, and usually the car is the most convenient place to do so. There are also some great apps out there that can record this stuff, just be sure to store your own data in case the app stops working for whatever reason.

Finally, set up a folder on your computer for tax records. Every time you receive an email with important information you need to keep for tax purposes, simply save the email in your tax records folder. Be as diligent as possible, because digging through old emails looking for a needle in a haystack can be tough, especially if you don't remember exactly what to search for.

That's pretty much it! Easy, right? We're only talking a few minutes a day, here and there. The biggest challenge is simply adjusting your daily habits to accommodate your tax record keeping. We know you can do it!

Now, the world isn't a perfect place, and mistakes happen, so let's talk about some tips. Plenty of retailers will email you a receipt, and they often ask if you would prefer that. Say yes (and get a printed receipt, too). We know why they offer this: they want to spam you with marketing material. Simply set up a "burner" email address like "catenthusiast99@fakemail.com" and have the receipts sent there. If you get a paper receipt as well, and use your envelopes, you might never need to check this email address, but it might save you if a receipt or two goes missing.

Wouldn't it be great to be able to know what IRS agents are looking for in an audit? Wouldn't it be even better to know what they're looking for when they audit your business in particular? What if you could see the questions they would ask? If you can believe it, all of this information is publicly available. Simply fire up your internet and search for "IRS Audit Techniques Guides." From there you can find the audit guide that applies to your business, and you can also take a look at the guide for "Activities not engaged in for profit" to see the data they will ask for when determining whether you're actually in business.

Hot Tax Tip
Take a look at the audit guide for your type of business. They're actually pretty easy to read and understand, and if anything scares you, then you know what to correct in your record keeping.

Finally, we generally recommend that you hire a qualified representative to help you if you're ever audited. Most audits are done via correspondence, believe it or not. The IRS sends the taxpayer a letter asking for some kind of documentation, the taxpayer supplies what the IRS needs, and that's the end of it. We certainly recommend that you utilize your tax professional to make sure you're handling this type of audit correctly. Sometimes the IRS requests to have a meeting, and in those cases it's best to have a tax professional handle the meeting for you. The first benefit is, you don't even need to attend! Imagine if you could hire someovne to stand in for you at your next root canal: wouldn't that be nice! Beyond that, your tax professional will be seasoned in handling these types of cases. They'll help get everything organized so that they can go through each document request and each question from the auditor completely and efficiently, without undersharing or oversharing. Your representative will also know your rights: he or she will know when to push back on requests and how to negotiate when it's appropriate.

Ultimately there is no such thing as "audit proofing" your tax return. You could get audited, and if that happens you will need solid books and records and experienced representation. However, after reading our book we hope you feel more comfortable that "solid records" can be easy to maintain, and experienced representation is as simple as hiring and retaining a good tax professional.

The home office explained: rules, strategies, best practices

What are the keys to the home office deduction? In order to claim an office in the home, it needs to be one of the following: a) your principal place of business, b) a place where you meet clients in the normal course of your business, c) a separate structure not attached to your residence, d) the area where you run a daycare business, or e) a place where you store inventory for sale.

"But wait, what does 'principal place of business mean?' That's really ambiguous." Agreed! Basically, it means the place where you conduct most of your business. If it's not the place you conduct most of your business (e.g. you're a rideshare driver) then it's the place where you do your administrative or management activities, and you don't have another office where you conduct these duties.

The space needs to be separate from other personal or living spaces. Usually that means it needs to be its own separate room, but a room divider can be used. Generally, common spaces like hallways and bathrooms are a no-no for the home office deduction.

You need to use the office regularly and exclusively for business. "Regularly" can mean a lot of different things for different people, and it's evaluated on a case-by-case basis by the IRS. With that in mind, we're not going to try to define "regularly" for you, but we will say that if you work at your business five days per week, then your home office probably won't pass an audit if you only use it one day per week.

"Exclusively" is easier to define, although it's important to note that this word "exclusively" doesn't apply to inventory storage or daycare businesses (so maybe it's not all that clear). Here's what you need to know: If your home office is your principal place of business, the place you meet clients, or a separate structure from your house, then you literally cannot use the space for anything non-business related. Don't put in a TV (unless it's critical for your business), and don't have non-business items like sports memorabilia, toys, books, magazines, or non-essential furniture in the area, either. A good rule of thumb is that if you get a business deduction for something, it can go in the home office. If it's not a deductible or depreciable business asset, get it out!

"What can I deduct in my home office?" Having a home office means you get to deduct some of your regular housing expenses against your business income. Things like property taxes, utilities, mortgage interest, and wifi can be allocated to their business use percentage and deducted against business income. Likewise, if you make any repairs or improvements to your home office, you can get a tax benefit for the full amount of the cash you spent. You can also deduct or depreciate the cost of the furniture and equipment you use in your home office. Finally, if you make any repairs or improvements to the home that affect the home office, you can deduct a portion of those. For example, if the roof covers the home office and you need a new one, you can deduct a portion of that expense because it indirectly benefits the office area. Ditto pest control and other indirect expenses.

Don't Go There Doug!

Doug's office has a big screen tv, a couch, a wet bar, a gaming system, and his racing simulator cockpit. Don't go there, Doug! If you don't use something for business, don't put it in your home office. Ok, if Doug is a famous streamer and makes a ton of money as he competes in simulated races before passing out on the couch, that's one thing (and even then this kind of business better be profitable otherwise it looks a lot like a hobby). In most cases? Don't go there, Doug!

"What can I not deduct in my home office?" Not every household expense can be attributed to the home office. For example, unless you're a swim instructor, it's not a good idea to allocate a portion of your pool maintenance to your home office. Likewise, if you remodel a bathroom that wouldn't count either, even if it's the bathroom you tend to use when working from home. Unless there is a direct link between a household expense and the home office, it's not deductible. For example, the home office uses electricity, therefore a portion of the electric bill is deductible because the electric bill is directly linked to the home office. However, when you make food in the kitchen and you eat it in the home office, that is not a direct link. Thus the cost of upgrading kitchen appliances is not a deductible home office expense.

Now, we're not attempting to describe every home office rule, and in some cases there are examples of when bathrooms, kitchens, and so on could be deductible. These nuances are a great reason why a good tax professional is so important!

You might be wondering, "How is the IRS going to know? Will they come to my house?" They can inspect your home office as part of their regular audit procedures, so play this one by the book.

"How can I make sure my home office will pass an audit?" That's easy! Use your home office regularly and exclusively for business, don't keep anything in there that isn't business related, and don't deduct inappropriate expenses. If the IRS believes one of the aforementioned rules was broken, they tend to disallow the entire home office. For example, if you have a table in your home office where your kids do their homework, the auditor is more likely to disallow your entire home office deduction than to simply reduce your deduction.

If you plan to remodel your home office to make it more suitable for meeting clients, or maybe you switch your home office from one room in the house to another, you should document the spaces before and after any changes. In this instance, it's a good idea to keep photographic evidence in your backup tax records.

Records Check
Remember that it's up to you to prove your tax deductions were proper. If you move, it's not like your home office deduction can never be challenged by the IRS. It's a good idea to keep photos of your office any time you change anything.

Can I make money from this? (or: How to construct a business model)

Maybe you have an idea for a business, and you're ready to get started putting things in motion. Before you invest too much time and money, we wholeheartedly recommend you put together a model of the business. What

Michael A. York, EA
Andrew L. Stevens, EA, MBA

is a business model anyway? A business model is just like those miniaturized architectural models of buildings you see before they break ground on a new development. In those architectural models they make a tiny representation of the actual building, the parking structure that goes with it, the entryway, the streets surrounding it, even down to the trees that will line the sidewalk. Why? Because before you commit to the real thing, it helps to understand how it will look and function when it's finished.

A business model does the same thing, but with numbers instead of styrofoam and paint. Most models are made in some kind of software like Excel, but many great businesses started on a bar napkin or the back of an envelope. We're not going to do a full Excel tutorial here, but it's an easy application to learn, and there are loads of lessons and tips online that will help you get started.

How do you get started, and how do you know when you're finished modeling a business? Start by making a very basic Profit and Loss (P&L) or "income" statement. This simple statement captures the performance of a business over a given timeframe starting with revenue, subtracting expenses, and ending up with profit. The timeframe can be a month or a quarter (three months), but it's usually a year, and most business models try to map out about five years of performance, showing revenue and expenses for each year so they can estimate how the business will grow and what kinds of expenses they can count on as they manage that growth.

"I'll just get started and figure out the rest as I go." Ok, awesome. Many great business people have done just that. But let's say you have two good ideas and you need to pick the better one, or let's say you're not that confident in your idea and you want to see how it might perform before you invest in it. A business model can answer a lot of questions, basically for free. It's also something you're going to need to have if you want to convince someone to give you money to get started. A model will help you figure out your breakeven price for your products or services, it will show you where your biggest expenditures are likely to be, and it will show you what big humps you will have to get over along the way.

> *Hot Tax Tip*
> A business model is a free way to get "under the hood" and see how a business works with zero cash and very little time invested!

As a personal note, once one of the authors was very close to investing his time and money in a startup that subleased cheap office space. It seemed like a very interesting idea, with little risk, very little start-up capital required, and potentially a nice profit potential. But after modeling the idea it became clear that the only way the business would be profitable in the long term was if Andy owned the building the office space was located in, which he did not. In this instance a quick modeling exercise saved a lot of time, money, and effort.

> *Records Check*
> Save every version of your business model as you create it and make changes. The metamorphosis it goes through can demonstrate to the IRS that you are changing your business plan to seek profitability.

How about one more great reason to construct a business model? The IRS loves them. One of the key things in the IRS audit guides, when auditing a business that might be a hobby, is whether or not there is a business plan. Now, our idea of a "business plan" is a 20-plus page document that explores the risks of a new endeavor, includes resumes and bios on the founders, shows the market and momentum of the product or service, and projects financials forward at least five years. The thing is, most of that information is only necessary if you seek investors. If you're financing a business out of your own savings, why would you write three pages about your own background?

Michael A. York, EA
Andrew L. Stevens, EA, MBA

Who are you trying to impress? However, projecting your financials forward shows the steps necessary to achieve a profit, like increasing revenue, cutting expenses, achieving economies of scale, etc. If you have a good business model to show an auditor, one that shows that you plan to make a profit in a certain year and you have plans for how to get there, then the auditor can check a box on his form and move on without asking for more information, which is exactly what you want to happen.

Conclusion – Until next time

Well, there you have it: We're done! We hope you will use this book as a reference when you're writing your own story – the one about how you started a business that helped secure your financial future and saved a little tax along the way. Whether you need to know specific details or understand a broader concept, we hope you find the answers here. If your questions are beyond the scope of this book, please call a qualified tax professional! You can also email us via our website at **www.notataxbook.com**. If there are enough unanswered questions, we might feel inspired to write a sequel.

Acknowledgements

Andy would like to thank his wife, Gowri, for her support, love, patience, and understanding. She's the ultimate partner in all things, and when she's not saving lives, she's the world's finest mom, teacher, and sleeper. She can also use one hand to push a stroller at high speed through a busy airport (which everyone should try at least once, just for a little humility). Thanks also to JayJay and our yet-unnamed daughter-to-be, for their daily inspiration, love, and for the gift of fatherhood, which is the greatest thing, ever. To my other better half, Michael, Andy would like to thank you for a lifetime of memories, even if I'm the sole owner of them. Andy would also like to thank his mom for letting us use her story, and for taking time away from her lucrative art business to read our tax book and give us feedback. The opportunity cost of the time she gave us is at least 10 *Hamilton* tickets.

Michael would like to thank Crystal, Caroline, Elizabeth, and Victoria, first and foremost. What an amazing, inspiring, strong, funny, loving, and overall BA life and business partner Crystal is, thank you for loving me. To my kiddos, I am so blessed to be your dad. Thank you for all the joy, love, snuggles, wrestle time, dance parties, adventures, and overall peace you guys bring every single day, thank you for being there. To my brother from another mother Andy, couldn't do it without you, thank you for all the love, logic, support, and friendship, love you man! To my in-laws, thank you for all the love and support. To Aline, wow, thank you, talented AF. Thank you to all of my amazing clients, another great day! Thank you to all of the people in my life that have taught me a thing or two, good, bad, and ugly it has all made me who I am today.

4am, Jack the Lion, Strictly Game, A&A, Kissing Families. I look forward to seeing you all at *Taxes the Musical - The Feelings of Taxes*, in the next decade or so. Love you, thank you, see you soon.

About the Authors

Andrew Stevens, EA, MBA is an experienced tax professional, entrepreneur, and corporate strategist. Prior to opening his practice in Houston, TX (www.houstontaxadvisors.com), he launched, managed, and sold a successful corporate team building and entertainment company. He has five years of experience as an M&A strategy consultant with Deloitte, specializing in post-merger integration, pre-deal screening, due diligence, and corporate restructuring, and he has served as a Director of Corporate Development and Due Diligence for a global telecom company. He brings nearly a decade of experience in the tax and financial planning business, and he earned a BS in Finance from the University of Utah, and an MBA from the Kenan-Flagler Business School at the University of North Carolina and IESE Business School in Barcelona, Spain.

Andy and his wife, Gowri, live in Houston, Texas where she practices medicine. They have a two year old son and a daughter is on the way.

Michael A. York, EA has spent his life in the tax business. Starting at 8 years old, he began helping in the family business, learning the ropes, and gaining experience on how to run a successful tax practice, which was in operation for 41 years. In 2016 he opened the doors to Michael A. York & Associates, LLC, a firm specializing in tax preparation and tax planning for individuals and small businesses (www.michaelayork.com). Since then he has spoken professionally on the topics of taxation issues for elders, retirement planning, small business tax strategies, and tax implications for high income salaried employees.

He and his wife, Crystal (who manages the firm's financial services practice), live in Salt Lake City, Utah with their three daughters.